mia culpa

Mia Freedman is a journalist, social commentator and blogger. She is the author of *Mama Mia* and blogs full time on her website, mamamia.com.au. She also chairs the National Body Image Advisory Group, with Sarah Murdoch, and appears regularly on the Today show.

mia culpa

mia freedman

VIKING
an imprint of
PENGUIN BOOKS

VIKING

Published by the Penguin Group
Penguin Group (Australia)
250 Camberwell Road, Camberwell, Victoria 3124, Australia
(a division of Pearson Australia Group Pty Ltd)
Penguin Group (USA) Inc.
375 Hudson Street, New York, New York 10014, USA
Penguin Group (Canada)
90 Eglinton Avenue East, Suite 700, Toronto, Canada ON M4P 2Y3
(a division of Pearson Penguin Canada Inc.)
Penguin Books Ltd
80 Strand, London WC2R 0RL, England
Penguin Ireland
25 St Stephen's Green, Dublin 2, Ireland
(a division of Penguin Books Ltd)
Penguin Books India Pvt Ltd
11 Community Centre, Panchsheel Park, New Delhi – 110 017, India
Penguin Group (NZ)
67 Apollo Drive, Rosedale, North Shore 0632, New Zealand
(a division of Pearson New Zealand Ltd)
Penguin Books (South Africa) (Pty) Ltd
24 Sturdee Avenue, Rosebank, Johannesburg 2196, South Africa

Penguin Books Ltd, Registered Offices: 80 Strand, London WC2R 0RL, England

First published by Penguin Group (Australia), 2011

1 3 5 7 9 10 8 6 4 2

Cover design by Nikki Townsend © Penguin Group (Australia)
Text design by Tony Palmer © Penguin Group (Australia)
Cover photograph by Jason Ierace/Fairfaxphotos
Typeset in 11.25/20pt Fairfield Light by Post Pre-press Group, Brisbane, Queensland
Printed and bound in Australia by McPherson's Printing Group, Maryborough, Victoria

National Library of Australia
Cataloguing-in-Publication data:

Freedman, Mia.
Mia Culpa / Mia Freedman.
9780670075515 (pbk.)
Women – Social conditions.

305.42

penguin.com.au

MIX
Paper from
responsible sources
FSC
www.fsc.org FSC® C001695

Contents

For Luca, Coco and Remy.

You are my trifecta

Introduction

I'm having two simultaneous and intense conversations in bed. One is with a close girlfriend. The other is with a woman I've never met. One woman is distressed, the other reflective. Both conversations are important. My husband is out for dinner and I'm relishing the opportunity to prop myself up on pillows, alone with my laptop, a packet of Smarties and a cup of tea.

My reflective friend has recently moved overseas and this is the only window when we're both awake and able to talk in real time, even though we're emailing. I miss her. She moved not for a job or a relationship but because she felt stuck. So six months ago, at 37, my friend impulsively decided to shake up her 'stagnant life', as she wryly described it.

Things were not going according to the unwritten plan she had in her head, a plan so ingrained in her expectations that it came as a rude shock that motherhood and a 'forever' relationship may never end up on her CV. Her actual CV is stellar, and for a while work was enough but not any more. 'I know everyone here,' she explained to her loved ones. 'I've done everything in this town. It's time.' And then she put her apartment on the market, sold her furniture on eBay and rolled the dice on a ticket to London where she had a few friends and a lead on a new job.

A routine pap smear had recently sparked a conversation with her doctor about fertility and on the eve of her 38th birthday she emailed to tell me that she's confronting some ugly statistics. After an initial freak-out, she's now trying to imagine what her life might look like without children in it and tentatively thinking that it might be okay. 'Or should I do the sperm bank thing?' she wonders, after taking me through some details about a disastrous date she'd been on last weekend. We discuss fertility options for a few emails and while I'm waiting for one of her replies, another email pops into my box from a name I don't instantly recognise.

Two women I know contacted me independently a few weeks ago within 24 hours of each other to ask for my advice for a friend who had just had a stillborn baby. Both women knew I'd lost a baby halfway through my second pregnancy and thought I might have some suggestions for what to do or say or send. Having experienced nothing similar themselves, they were lost. I guessed that they were asking about the same women and after linking them to a couple of articles I've published on Mamamia about pregnancy loss and still-birth, I asked for their friend's email.

I don't know exactly why. I just felt compelled to be in touch with her. Possibly because I remembered how through my fog of grief for months afterwards, it was somehow easier to talk to strangers than the people who loved me most.

That was unexpected because I've always been very close to my friends. But during those dark, dark months, the only people I wanted to talk to were those who had been through something similar. Except I couldn't find them because it was before the Internet had permeated our lives. Impulsively I'd emailed this woman a day ago and now she's replied.

It's an intensely moving exchange as I tell her things about my lost daughter, May, that I've never told anyone, not even my husband. She responds with intimate confessions of her own and as my other girlfriend logs off to go to work, this stranger and I continue to email for an hour, making each other smile and cry with black grief and even blacker humour. Until she isn't a stranger any more. I don't know if we'll ever meet. I hope so. But we'll be forever connected regardless through shared memories of the daughters we never got to take home.

It occurs to me that the computer has joined cocktails, coffee and cake as fundamental conduits to female conversations. Not that we require conduits. Put any two women within two metres of each other and you have an instant water cooler. Sometimes, when I meet someone new and I tell them I'm a writer, they ask, 'What do you write about?' Tricky question. It's a lot like asking a woman who just came home from a girls' dinner, 'What did you talk about?'. The short answer? EVERYTHING.

An average conversation between two women will move seamlessly from politics to the difference between postnatal depression and the baby blues, how you should go up a cup size when ordering bras from Victoria's Secret online to hangover cures to controlled crying to the perils of going to IKEA alone to interest rates to Facebook to managing anxiety to childcare to sex to Bonds tracksuit pants to Gwyneth to refugees to orange lipstick to broadband to Botox to pelvic floor exercises . . . and that just about covers the first cocktail. Often, when I'm catching up with a girlfriend I haven't seen for a while, we joke that we need a written agenda, a PowerPoint presentation and a laser pointer to make sure we don't miss any vital installments of information.

But blokes seem to be able to spend hours and hours talking about . . . Well, I have no idea what they talk about because they rarely seem to have retained any of it by the time they get home. When my husband comes home from a night out with his friends, the conversation usually goes something like this.

'So, was Johno there?'

'Yeah, he was actually.'

'And how's Ava?'

Blank.

'You know, Johno and Benita's baby?'

'Um . . .' I can tell he's stalling, waiting for the right answer to fall from the sky into his head. 'Her hip. Remember, she had to have it put in plaster to correct that dysplasia thing?'

'Uh, I guess she's fine. Johno didn't say anything.'

'What about Sandra? Did she end up resigning after that thing at the Christmas party? Did Phil say?'

'Ah, no . . . I don't think he mentioned it.'

'Are Parky and Joanna back together? Have Craig and Margie decided to do another round of IVF? Has Chopper come out to his boss at work? Did Spud's apartment sell at auction? That girl that Sam met on the Internet – what was her name? Shani, did that work out? Oh, and Craig's Mum – is she out of hospital?'

Blankety blank blank blank.

'Babe, you know what it's like. We just didn't talk about any of that stuff.' He shrugs.

But I can't let it go. 'What DID you talk about then? Surely in five hours you have to exchange SOME information about SOMEthing? Tell me one new thing you learned.'

Pause. Thinks. A flash of relief.

'Craig's got a new car. A Peugeot.'

'That's it?'

'That's it.'

I know a mountain of intimate details about the lives of women I barely know.* I know that one of my children's teachers has a sister with depression and is sometimes bedridden for weeks. I know that the woman who runs my

---

* I've changed a couple of details here to protect the privacy of these women and their families . . .

local coffee shop has had six miscarriages and has finally given up hope of ever becoming a biological mother. She's investigating adoption and we've discussed which countries allow single women to adopt. I know intimate details about my hairdresser's cycle and the various hits and misses she's had with different forms of contraception. I know that the husband of one of my child's school friends has a drinking problem. I know that another mother is in recovery from an eating disorder. I know that a woman who gave me a massage one time had just lost her elderly father and was fighting with her estranged brother over the will. And none of these people are even my friends. The things I know about my friends and their loved ones could fill this book twenty times over. And they know just as much about me.

Sharing information is what women do. It's how we process our lives, by presenting them to others for input, for empathy or just to hear ourselves speak them out loud. I've come to the conclusion that it's rooted in the primitive female need to gather. While cavemen hunted meat, cavewomen gathered salad. They also gathered information because they had lots of time to talk while sitting around sorting bush leaves and preparing roast mammoth. But hunting? That required silence. A lot like watching cricket.

As my husband observed, 'When you talk as much as women do, you need to have an enormous amount of information on hand.' That's why, when the roles are reversed and I come home after dinner with girlfriends, my husband is cautious about expressing too much interest in what was discussed. He keeps his questions broad and non-specific. Or pretends to be asleep. Because it would take hours to download what I'd just uploaded and he wouldn't remember it by the morning anyway. It's not that he doesn't adore my friends; he just has a limited capacity to retain the details.

But it's different for me. I live for details. Connecting with my friends and diving into the minutiae of our lives is like a mix of caffeine with a chamomile chaser. Energising and soothing. Intense and reassuring. All the anecdotes in this book are drawn from such conversations so it's probably a good time to thank them for their candour. And then run for cover . . .

Does My Bum Look Old in This?

Pubic hair is sooo last year. In fact, it may even be as retro as the year before, which means it's practically extinct. I am reliably informed of this by several different sources and absolutely no scientific research whatsoever.

My benign interest in this subject was initially sparked when I heard a guy casually make the following remark at a barbecue: 'You know, it's the strangest thing. No one under thirty has pubic hair any more.'

As far as small talk goes, this was certainly a little left of centre. And it made a refreshing change from your standard social chitchat about interest rates and reality TV. So with the kids playing out of earshot, a small crowd gathered around, sausages and wine in hand, to discuss the mysterious disappearance of pubic hair on a generation of sexually active adults. Poof. Gone.

It turns out the guy who started the conversation came to his conclusion after clocking an enormous amount of time watching YouPorn, the site where regular people upload clips of themselves doing rude things with other consenting adults. Nobody on YouPorn, it seems, has pubic hair. 'It's all gone,' he said, shaking his head in bewilderment. 'Even the blokes don't have any.'

At this, gasps were heard in the crowd as a disturbing mental picture flashed across everyone's mind. The men imagined themselves pube-less. The women imagined the men. Brows furrowed collectively in dismay and confusion . . . *but why would you?*

Since no one at the barbecue could shed further light on the subject, our questions remained unanswered.

And since *Four Corners* was unable to launch an immediate investigation, I was forced to make my own inquiries. Was this mass deforestation a mere quirk of freaky people who like to film themselves having sex and share it online?

Over the following weeks, I established some compelling anecdotal evidence to the contrary. It appears it's not just amateur porn stars and celebutantes who are going totally bare down there. It's an epidemic.

Anecdote One: I suddenly remembered a conversation I'd had with a colleague several months ago. The woman's daughter was seventeen and she wanted to have everything lasered off. When her mother expressed dismay that she would opt for such a permanent form of hair removal she might later regret, the daughter was baffled. 'But, Mum,' she sighed, rolling her eyes. 'Why would I ever want *pubic hair*?' in the same tone of voice she might have said 'herpes'. Fortunately, the salon she went to had a no-bikini-lasering-under-eighteen policy for this exact reason: teenagers and the idea of permanence are strangers. So she went for the full wax instead, just like all her friends.

Anecdote Two: Over dinner with some people I didn't know very well, the extinction of pubic hair on my mind, I broke the ice by asking if anyone had firsthand knowledge of blokes waxing, lasering or shaving below the waist. 'As a matter of fact, a couple of my mates do it,' said one guy, before insisting he himself did not. Cough. So why did his mates? 'They say it's for two reasons. One is that it's a sign of respect to the girl. You know, if she waxes, he's willing to as well. And they also say it makes them look bigger.' Hands up who thinks the first reason is a furphy? Me too.

Anecdote Three: A married friend recently went for her usual bikini wax. Nothing fancy. Just so she can wear a swimming costume to the beach and not be mistaken for a yeti. The beautician was telling her an involved story about some guy who'd stood her up and my friend was trying to focus on the story instead of the pain, which seemed to be worse than normal.

Suddenly, the beautician paused mid-sentence and held her wax spatula aloft. 'You usually have it all off, don't you?' she asked by way of confirmation.

'Uh, no!' my friend exclaimed, glancing downwards and trying not to freak out at what she saw. Or rather, what she didn't see.

The beautician laughed nervously. 'Oops. I'm sorry about that but it's all gone! Ha, ha, ha. I'm so used to doing a full wax, I was on autopilot! I hardly ever get requests to leave anything any more, not even a landing strip. Sorry again. Oh well, makes a change for you, I guess. Something different.'

And with that, my friend was left unintentionally bald. Bald and displeased. 'I have a nine-year-old daughter,' she huffed to me afterwards. 'Why the hell would I want to look like my child? It's sick. What's wrong with people that they'd want to look like that?'

I'm not sure why pubic hair exists due to my extreme aversion to typing those two words into Google. You understand. Suffice to say it's there for a number of very good reasons we don't need to explore now or possibly ever. So what will be the long-term ecological effect of this unnatural land-clearing in a generation of lady gardens and man parts?

You might want to give that some thought next time you're lying half naked on a table while a stranger shoots a laser gun at your vagina. As laser treatments become more popular for bikini lines, suddenly hair removal has become all *Sex and the City* meets *Star Wars*. Nude from the waist down.

According to a recent university study, 61 per cent of women say they do activities they don't enjoy in order to improve their looks. Clearly, the other 39 per cent are either nuns or liars.

With the exception of a haircut, there's not much about maintaining your looks that doesn't hurt if you're female. And since the amount of upkeep required to look decent increases with every passing year, so does the pain. Beauty hurts.

I sometimes think men have rather a wafty idea of what

goes on in beauty salons. It's certainly not their fault. The name 'beauty salon' has misleading connotations of pampering. It implies fluffy white towels, soothing strokes and Norah Jones music. But last time I checked, being plucked, squeezed, peeled, lasered, ripped and tweezed with or without hot wax being poured directly onto your genitals is not most girls' idea of a pampery good time.

Sadly, it's not just hair removal that hurts. Massages notwithstanding, most things that happen at a beauty salon tend to be ouchy. Like 'extraction' or 'cleaning'. This is beauty-speak for squeezing the bejesus out of your face. And 'brow-shaping', which involves an unsoothing combination of hot wax and tweezers. And peels. This is a lot like pouring acid onto your face, and then leaving it there until you're desperate to slam your hand in a car door just TO TAKE YOUR MIND OFF YOUR FACE PAIN.

Even the hairdresser is not pain free. This is a surprising truth I learnt in 1990 when Yazz was cool (The only way is up. Ba-by. Remember?), and I bleached my short hair white. Imagine a thousand bees all over your scalp, stinging you at once. For an hour. Good times.

And now we have laser. I'm not sure why the torture of waxing or the hassle of shaving had to be superseded by something that involves eye-protection goggles and the smell of burning hair. But there you go. We'll do anything and pay anyone who will promise us flawlessness or hairlessness. We are that easy.

Really, we shouldn't complain. Complaining should be the exclusive right of those who go to hospital after a beauty treatment. According to the Accident Research Centre at Monash University, ninety Victorians were hospitalised last year with waxing injuries. One of them was a diabetic woman who experienced a life-threatening infection after some minor bleeding following her treatment with a trainee waxer. I'd hazard a guess that her big mistake can be found in the last two words of the preceding sentence: trainee waxer. Look, I'm sure trainee waxers do need to practise but couldn't they do it on, say, themselves?

According to newspaper reports, 'Within a fortnight, the diabetes sufferer, who has a lowered immune system, was suffering excruciating pain, a fever and a rash extending to her chest, arms and neck. Doctors at the Austin Hospital unit saved her life with antibiotics.'

So who are we suffering for exactly? Rarely, it seems, men. I don't know many guys who have rolled over after a particularly nice shag and remarked, 'You know, babe?

With smaller pores and more streamlined eyebrows, that sex would have been even better!'

It's not really about men. This is confirmed by a quick poll of Brazilian devotees (those who seek to remove their 'undercarriage' of pubic hair, if not the whole lot). These are women who have been committed to the torture for years, even through periods of deliberate celibacy and relationships with men who couldn't care if they had bubble wrap or silver tinsel down there. 'I do sometimes ask myself why I'm doing it,' admits one happily single Brazilian-ed friend in her mid-forties. 'I've concluded it's a form of voluntary masochism. I just like the way it looks.'

Also taking a keen interest in voluntary masochism are men. A few years ago, men started getting their backs waxed. Now it's laser. When I went to get my legs lasered recently, I counted four men in the waiting room, aged about twenty-five to forty.

The beautician told me half her clients were men and some had begun to request a 'Manzilian' – the complete removal of all hair down there. 'They've tried waxing it off but the in-growns are a killer,' she explained. Indeed they can be, something women have known since the dawn of waxing.

But why are these men doing it? *Why?*

'Some say it makes sex better and that their partners prefer it. Others say that without all the extra foliage, the tree trunk looks bigger.'

Ah yes. That again. Whether you're male or female, vanity plays an enormous part in how much pain we're willing to endure. 'I want to look the very best I can, and the older you get the more it all hurts,' says a friend in her thirties who has some kind of beauty treatment every second week. 'It's all horribly unpleasant but absolutely necessary.'

'The worst and most humiliating beauty treatment is tattoo removal,' insists another friend, who knows this to be true. In 1992, after a bad break-up, she had a small tattoo applied to her right buttock for $50. She was twenty and thought it looked beautiful. 'Fifteen years and eight removal treatments at $150 each later, I am living proof that not only does beauty hurt but it is indeed in the eye of the beholder. And it's bloody expensive.'

Generally, I find that the more disfigured you look after a beauty treatment – greasy hair, squeezed skin, ugly red marks on your face where your eyebrows used to be – the more likely it is that you will bump into an ex-boyfriend.

As unfortunate as this may be, if you were in a long-term relationship with said ex, that might be exactly how he remembers you.

Picture this. With spring in the air and summer on the horizon, you glance down in the shower one day and realise it's time to mow the lawn. 'Goodness,' you exclaim, 'I really should do something about my bikini line.' Wandering past the bathroom, your partner shoots back drily, 'What bikini line?'

This actually happened to me recently and it seems to be a rather common exchange – even if it doesn't always occur out loud.

In most cases, there's a direct correlation between the amount of time you've been with someone and the amount of effort you put into personal grooming. The words 'inversely proportional' spring to mind.

Remember that old joke about the bride with the big smile walking down the aisle? The punch line – 'She's smiling because she's given her last blow job' – could just as easily be recast as 'because she never has to have another Brazilian'.

There are two things that deplete a woman's interest in hair removal: winter and love. Not new, buzzy love but years and years of the comfortable-and-secure kind. The more of it you have, the less hair you feel compelled to remove.

As the years pass, you trade that buzzy feeling for something deeper; knowing you're loved for who you really are, no trimmings necessary. But there's a line between feeling secure and just . . . letting it all hang out. Or, in many cases, grow out.

And it goes both ways. 'Last week, my husband asked how much longer I was planning on letting my winter coat grow,' grumbled one friend. 'My response was to snap back about a new phenomenon sweeping the world called "manscaping".'

When I asked a bunch of women aged twenty-six to forty-five about how romantic status affects grooming, I received some honest responses. 'I used to want to be all smooth and pristine for my husband but now I figure he's lucky to get any, and he isn't going to complain about petty details like furry legs or an overgrown bikini line,' replied one woman. 'And guess what? He doesn't.'

Or as another woman put it: 'I don't call it "letting myself go", I call it "contraception".'

That noise you can hear is the sound of personal grooming standards whizzing down past your ears somewhere around the two- to five-year mark. You would not believe what occurs in some long-term relationships. Or maybe you would because your own standards are similarly slip-sliding away.

Like the woman who goes to sleep each night wearing nose-pore strips. Or the couple who floss their teeth together *in bed*. 'I mean, that's the beginning of the end really, isn't it?' acknowledges the female half of that couple. 'How do you make love to someone after you've watched them examine what comes out of the crevices between their teeth?'

Somewhere between the first time he sees you naked and happily-ever-after, some women discover their motivation to look good shifts from pleasing him to pleasing others. 'I shave my legs for my physio, not my boyfriend,' noted one woman. 'I only bother with nice undies when I have a gyno appointment,' admitted another. 'I never wear make-up unless I'm going out with my girlfriends,' concurred a third.

Like Brazilians, fancy underwear seems to be an early casualty of marriage. 'I used to wear matching lingerie pretty much every day,' mused one friend. 'These days, do old black Bonds hipsters and a black maternity bra count?' (Not really, although I maintain birth exempts you from all personal grooming for at least a year, possibly two.)

Interestingly, many women are reminded to lift their game by children not partners. 'I only remember to shave my legs when my three-year-old tells me I'm spiky,' remarks one. 'I still wear a little bit of make-up every day but it's so I don't embarrass the kids when I'm in the school playground,' agrees another.

My son said to me today, 'Mum, I can see your wrinkles. They're worse in the morning. You should put some cream on them.'

I probably should. As I get older, I edge ever closer to that perennial question: which do you choose – face or ass? Ladies, nature will force you to make this choice about your appearance, as you get older. And gentlemen? I'm sure you've already made it in terms of the female aesthetics you prefer.

The theory behind this dilemma – first identified by Mae West in the 1930s – is quite simple. Oh, and sexist, naturally. Because for the purpose of this argument, one has to assume the definition of a 'good' ass is 'firm and compact' and a 'good' face is one that looks youthful.

And here lies the problem. A 'good' ass requires a low percentage of body fat. But as you age, a 'good' face needs a higher amount of body fat to fill out lines and wrinkles.

This is the *Sophie's Choice* of female vanity: face or ass. Oh, whatever shall we do?

Well, if you're fond of a needle, there's always the option of injecting your ass *into* your face and killing two birds with one syringe. That's the approach taken by many female celebrities over thirty, because they can. It doesn't even have to be your *own* ass! Isn't that just so great! If you've already starved and dieted your ass into oblivion so you can slip into those size 0 designer frocks, you can just inject some synthetic ass – I mean fat – into the lines on your face.

But this is cheating. And unnatural. And a bit nauseating to think about. For the rest of us, the choice must be made. Perhaps you've already made it.

I have a friend with an extremely small and firm ass. She is a yoga nut and does Ashtanga for two hours every morning. She also plays tennis and swims laps of her local beach.

I've always admired her dedication to exercise, while secretly coveting her ass. But lately, as she sun salutes her way towards forty, I've noticed she's starting to look old. Older than her age. At first I wondered if I was being unfair. Or jealous. Maybe she was just tired. But I met up with her for breakfast last month and, in the morning light, I got quite a shock. My gorgeous friend is still gorgeous, but her face is beginning to look, well, I wish there was a word other than haggard but that's the one that popped into my head at the time.

Her body doesn't look unhealthy, just hard. But her face? It's obviously drawn the short straw in this particular bargain and her firm bottom has assumed the power position. I found myself ordering French toast just to reaffirm my face choice. Suddenly, I didn't envy her ass any more.

Since that breakfast, I've become curious about the choices other women have made. 'I've started using SPF 30+ every day and I've let my gym membership lapse,' notes one 38-year-old friend. 'I guess that means I've chosen my face.'

Another friend, thirty-four, explains her face choice like this: 'People look at your face all day, but they only look at your ass if it's particularly hot or if you're wearing a G-string at the beach. Also, you can dress in a way that minimises your ass problem, but there's no hiding your face unless you wear a burqa.'

Sometimes, nature chooses for you. Laments one 46-year-old woman I know: 'It's true that my round face makes me look younger than my skinny sister, even though I'm actually six years older, but it's definitely not a choice I've made. I'm always trying for a skinny ass but as I get older I start to look more like my mum, who's pear-shaped. My chest is growing at the same rate as my ass though, so for my husband that's a bonus. Even without the big boobs, he says he'd choose a bit of padding over a wrinkled face.'

So would most men, I think. We tend to place far too much importance on the small-ass thing when men are far more accepting and embracing of our asses. So to speak.

'For me, a happy face is everything,' agrees yet another friend who has chosen upstairs over downstairs. 'That drawn, thin look is incredibly aging. I mean, show me a female runner who looks younger than they are? Just doesn't happen. But show me a woman who eats, drinks and laughs a lot and it will all be there on her face, and she will likely be beautiful, no matter what her age.'

Anyway, skinny girls are liars. The only way a woman past puberty can be thin is via anorexia or bulimia or drugs. But do they admit this? They do not. Instead, they lie. They say, '*I don't have an eating disorder.*' Oh puh-lease! They say, '*I eat all the time!*' Pah! They say, '*My mother is skinny too, it's genetics.*' Give me a break! They say, '*I try to put on weight but I can't.*' Yeah, right . . .

And do we believe them? Hell to the no. We sneer and we snark and we roll our eyes because they are liars, aren't they? *Aren't they?*

Well, maybe they aren't. Maybe, just maybe, some women are naturally thin, in the same way that some women, no matter how much they diet and exercise, are naturally large. Or curvy. Or tall.

So why do so many women feel so suspicious and hostile towards our skinny sisters? Jealousy, perhaps. We envy their willpower, their ability to eat cake without fear or consequence, their fast metabolism and their teeny tiny bottoms. Is that it?

I have a girlfriend who is very thin. She also has four kids. This rare combination means she's constantly on the receiving end of veiled accusations disguised as faux concern. 'I'm constantly being asked, "Do you ever eat?"' she sighs, 'even by people I've just met or the guy who makes my coffee. One of my friends is obese and can barely carry her own toddler. I would never comment on her weight or say I was worried about her health, and yet she feels perfectly comfortable introducing me to people as "my hungry friend". She thinks it's funny.'

My skinny friend (who is not, in fact, hungry) also has to

deal with constantly being told, 'You don't look like you have four kids!' To this, she replies, 'No one sent me the memo advising that you have to be a certain size to be a mother.'

There are very few people we're allowed to be horrible about any more. This is a good thing. We've learnt (well, most of us have learnt) that it's unacceptable to insult people based on their race, gender, height, age or size – not if they're overweight, anyway.

But somehow, skinny women fell through the cracks. Maybe because they're so skinny – get it! Ha ha. See, there you go, that's a perfect example of an insidious trend: Skinny Bashing. Can you imagine me making a joke about fat people? I never would. But skinny people get no such protection, no such social courtesy because . . . they're skinny. It seems to be as simple as that.

I used to be a skinny basher. My intentions were good but I was still guilty. A decade ago when I was a magazine editor, in an attempt to redress the appalling imbalance of female body shapes in magazines, I began to feature larger girls in fashion stories. Emboldened, I also started to run features declaring that men preferred 'real women with real curves' instead of 'a bag of bones'. This was not very empowering for thin women, however. It was insulting. Demonising one body shape in favour of another or labelling one type of woman 'real' and another 'fake' doesn't advance the cause of body acceptance; it just shifts the target of discrimination.

After being told this loudly by dozens of thin women who wrote me abusive letters, I quickly adjusted my message and my thinking. Diversity is key in the media. All sizes and skin colours can be attractive and desirable.

However, sometimes I think we walk a fine line between body image and obesity. I'm often asked if the idea of having more diversity in the way women are portrayed in the media is simply promoting obesity.

Please.

There is a massive gap between size 6 and obese. But it's a gap that's glaringly ignored when it comes to women in magazines, on catwalks and in advertisements. It's also important to acknowledge that, sometimes, people *want* to lose weight. Sometimes, they *need* to lose weight.

So how do you tell someone they're too fat? Really, how do you say those words to a friend or a lover? And too fat for what exactly? Their health? Your eyes? Skinny jeans?

I started thinking about the touchy subject of weight discussions one day after I had coffee with a girlfriend. 'I've put on so much weight lately,' she sighed as we drank soy lattes.

'No you haven't!' I replied automatically because that's what friends do. But I wasn't being disingenuous. I never notice what my friends weigh. I simply don't see it. If you asked me to describe any of them, a weight word wouldn't make it into my top ten adjectives.

Others, however, do notice when loved ones gain weight and choose to comment. Some even live to tell the tale.

When I asked about weight interventions on Twitter, I spent an entertaining hour fielding dozens of replies. Julie said, 'Husband bringing it up on Mother's Day, "Have you put on weight?", is a definite fail. And punch in the head.' Lily said, 'It's tricky. "I'm worried about you" is a good start to the conversation in our house.' Mel said, 'I asked for a massage and got a Wii Fit. Clearly, husband trying to tell me something.' Katrina said, 'If my girlfriend is looking fat, I'll tell her and expect her to do the same, so it's not off limits for us, but we're lesbians!'

Among hetero couples, weight discussions are higher risk. Most men live in fear of their partner faux-casually dropping the killer question: 'Honey, do you think I've put on weight?' Accepted wisdom dictates one correct answer: 'No' – said quickly with conviction and a splash of shock. But what if the answer is yes? Why is honesty about this subject so taboo?

Of course, when someone you love is dangerously over-weight and risking their health, the stakes are higher than hurt feelings. At myfatspouse.org, a site *'for discussions about obesity and relationships'*, the advice is to tread carefully. *'Attempting to change a wife or husband's behaviour ranks up there with "Let's invade Russia" on the stupid-idea list. Your attempt may very well backfire, and it's likely you'll end up with an angry and fat spouse.'*

Back to my friend and our soy lattes. She was neither fat nor angry, although she did insist she'd put on about six kilograms since the previous winter. 'The other day I was grumbling about how my legs looked like sausages and Ben said, "Yes, darling, they do a bit, and actually, I seem to have stacked it on too. Shall we go back to pilates together again?"'

When my friend told me this story with an easy laugh, I was struck by how rare it is for a man to be able to answer a question about his partner's weight honestly without trigger-ing an emotional meltdown. Not that every man who replies, 'Oh noooo, your bum doesn't look big' is lying but hey, some of them are.

And they lie because we make them. When we ask, 'Have I put on weight?' what we're really asking for is reassurance that we haven't, truth be damned. Men understand this and they comply.

For them, it's different. Telling a man he's gained weight registers about the same low frequency on the self-worth indicator as telling a woman, 'Gee, your hair's got long.' He may not greet the news with a happy jig but it's unlikely to send him into a spiral of self-loathing. There will rarely be tears or slammed doors. He won't go on a sex strike. Mostly, he'll just grab a handful of gut, shake his head a bit to process the information, and then either do something about it or ignore you.

But women? Like, whoa. Tell us we've gained weight and watch us shout or cry or go really, really quiet. We'll prickle with shame or embarrassment and we'll feel terrible about ourselves.

The reason men have learnt to be so fearful around the subject of our weight is because, unfortunately, our body image is so often interwoven with our sense of self. This is why we tend to announce, 'I feel so fat!' when fat is not technically a feeling.

Remember that the next time you 'feel' fat because what you're feeling is something else. Boredom, frustration, anger, disappointment, despair, depression, loneliness – all feelings. Fat? That's a description. You can't feel it.

The weight conversation between my friend and her partner was refreshing because he respected her enough to be honest and she respected herself enough not to freak out. It was an observation not an indictment and she recognised it as such, knowing that her self-worth doesn't live in her muffin.

Still, all this male–female complexity sometimes makes me yearn for a simpler dynamic. Like the one Katrina has with her girlfriend. Or the one between male friends. As one guy replied to me on Twitter: 'It's easy between blokes. We just say, "Shit, you've got fat, mate."'

I do love the ability men have to just cut to the chase, which is why I was alarmed when it seemed like male botox could become a trend. Thankfully, this didn't seem to eventuate, but botox for women keeps chugging along and gaining momentum.

One day not long ago, I was sitting in the waiting room at the dermatologist's office, while the receptionist was talking on the phone to a patient who was trying to make an appointment.

The only reason I was eavesdropping – I mean listening – is because I am shamelessly nosy. It was also because the newest magazine in the waiting room was from 2007. I resolved in that moment that if I become any type of doctor in the future, I will stock the latest magazines in my waiting room and write them off as tax deductions. After I've read them.

That decided, my eyes and ears had been flitting around the room urgently looking for distraction. I found it in the form of the receptionist's conversation, which would have been utterly unremarkable were it not for what I heard next. 'Can I just get your name?' the receptionist asked the caller. She then repeated the name, which I immediately recognised as a high-profile colleague in the fashion industry. Someone I respected and admired.

'Right, and what's the appointment for?' Pause. 'Botox? Okay.'

At this point I thought my ears might fall off with excitement. The receptionist continued. 'Now, of course you know how it all works from the other times, but just remember to arrive an hour early to have the numbing cream applied. Terrific, see you tomorrow at 10.30.'

This woman coming to get her face jabbed – evidently not for the first time – is very beautiful. I've always thought so and I've never been able to pick her age. Forty-something, perhaps.

Once the thrill of this illicit information subsided, I spent the rest of my time in the waiting room thinking about botox and sifting through my conflicting feelings on the subject.

It's probably worth mentioning at this point that I was not at the dermatologist for botox. Never had it. In fact, on good days, I can get very high-horsey about it. 'Why are we turning ourselves into a generation of Stepford Wife clones?' I'll rage to anyone who's listening and also those who don't care. 'Why are we erasing our facial expressions with needles and poison? What message are we sending to our daughters? That female beauty is based on a blank face? Honestly! *Appalling! Appalling!*'

I also remind myself that I got my laugh lines from laughing. And that that's a good thing.

But on bad days, days when I'm feeling old and wrinkly, I look in the mirror, stumble off my soapbox and shrug, 'Oh, whatever. Maybe I should. Anything to make me look less tired.' While I haven't yet waved the white flag and succumbed to the jab, it's mildly disturbing to me that my feminist principles can be supplanted so easily by vanity. Even if it's just for a weak moment.

Evidently, I'm not getting younger. I was reminded of this a few months ago when I received a call from a sub-editor at a magazine who rang to check my age for a story. Here's what I've noticed about telling someone your age: part of you dearly wants the reply to be: 'My goodness! You don't look it!'

However, that's not quite the response I got when I told this woman how old I was. 'Oh yeah,' she said with audible smugness. 'A few of us here were looking at your photo and we guessed that.' Oh. That's okay, I reassured my botox-free self. And it was okay. Until she hit me with the sting: 'I hate to tell you but you look your age.'

Ouch. Waddya say to that, huh? What indeed. Look, I think I can quite reasonably deal with looking my age. But it was the way she said, 'I hate to tell you . . .' as if she were breaking some terribly bad news to me.

Look, it's not the numbers that are bothering me as I get older so much as the utter lack of visual role models. Possibly, my big mistake in my thirties – heck, at any age – has been to unwittingly reference myself against celebrities. Silly, silly me. Stupid, idiot me. Because lately, celeb magazines are starting to resemble cyborg catalogues. None of the women in them looks remotely human. And once you factor in their ages, your brain starts to hurt with the effort of reconciling what you know about aging with what you are seeing.

There are celebrities who are older than me in years but look younger. Much younger. This is confusing. There are also celebrities who used to be older than me, or the same age, but are now younger. Or claim to be. This, too, is confusing. But the truly disconcerting thing is that group of famous women (and a few famous men) who look like cyborgs. Often you can't put your finger on just what's wrong with their faces but their resemblance to the human form is . . . long gone.

Is this the ultimate achievement? Transcending the ageing process by becoming alien? These are usually the celebrities who, in interviews, coyly claim never to have had plastic surgery because, 'Personally, I could just never do it, you know?' They will then add carefully, 'But I wouldn't judge anyone who did.' Oh no. Of course you wouldn't.

My biggest issue is with the lies – not just from celebrities but from the magazines themselves.

I recently stumbled across a photo of Cindy Crawford in the nude. No, it wasn't a men's mag but a beauty mag, because sometimes it seems there are just as many naked and semi-naked women in magazines aimed at women. Go figure.

Anyway, there was Cindy wearing a full face of make-up

and some strategically placed shaving cream. The former supermodel looked exactly as you'd expect. Stunning. Sudsy. Whatever. But what troubled me – deeply – was the headline next to naked Cindy.

'**THIS IS WHAT 43 LOOKS LIKE**' it declared. Like hell it is. The caption underneath read:

'*Cindy Crawford's skin-care regimen includes a day cream with antioxidants, a sunscreen, a night cream and an eye cream.*'

This would be fine had Cindy herself not admitted years ago in interviews that she first saw a cosmetic surgeon aged twenty-nine, and that 'creams work on the texture of your skin but to restore elasticity, I count on botox, collagen and vitamin injections. I drink a lot of water, watch what I eat and exercise. But I owe the quality of my skin to my cosmetic surgeon.'

Honesty points to Cindy. Such disclosure is rare. And an artfully extended middle finger to *Allure* magazine for failing to mention the cosmetic surgery, airbrushing the shot to oblivion and then pretending the result was achieved with a sprinkling of antioxidants.

When I posted the Cindy photo and an accompanying rant on my website, comments exploded. Women were exasperated at yet another example of media hypocrisy. Men were exasperated too. By the women. They couldn't understand why we were kicking up a stink. Typical of this sentiment was a guy who wrote: 'What is it with women and rubbishing other women who are better looking than them? Yeah, no shit, Cindy Crawford looks good at forty-three – she's a supermodel. *Allure* is obviously trying to sell products, not report the news. Derr! Who cares if she's had stuff done?'

I've heard this argument many times from men, and while I understand their frustration, they're missing the point. We're not rubbishing women who are better looking than us. We don't resent them for it; in fact, we can appreciate and celebrate female beauty as enthusiastically as men. This is not about jealousy. It's not even about cosmetic surgery. That's a personal decision between a woman and her mirror.

This is about *deception*. When celebrities and magazines claim the secret to flawless beauty and a hot body is confidence and some sunscreen, we know it's poppycock. And that's even before the image is heavily photoshopped, transforming it into something that appears human but isn't. 'Why do you care?' exclaim men. 'Why do you compare? JUST. STOP.' Excellent suggestion. If only it was so simple.

Let's play pretend for a moment.

Pretend the world was full of pictures of naked men. On billboards and the sides of buses, in magazines and ads for beer, cars and deodorant. Imagine there were penises everywhere you turned and you couldn't escape seeing them every day.

And *all* the images of nude men were fake. Every male model and celebrity had had penile enlargement surgery, and afterwards, his penis had been extensively photoshopped to make it look even bigger. So now, all the penises you saw in the media every day were knee-length and as thick as an arm.

One day, next to a magazine article about a celebrity with a foot-long penis, you read the headline: '**This is what a 43-year-old penis looks like.**' The caption underneath read: '*Asked for the secret to his long shlong, former male model Marcus Schenkenberg insists he was just born that way. "I wear cotton boxer shorts and I exfoliate in the shower," he shrugs. "That's all I do."*'

After reading a hundred stories like that and being bombarded by 10 000 images of men with surgically altered and digitally enhanced penises, do you think you might look down at your natural, un-photoshopped trouser snake and feel a little . . . deflated? Inadequate? Insecure? Angry?

Because that's exactly what it's like to be a woman in today's media landscape. You don't have to be a fashion victim or a magazine junkie to be bombarded by images of women who have been surgically enhanced and drastically photoshopped. You can't escape the pop-culture wallpaper of it unless you hide under the bed with your eyes shut, which tends to be a little impractical.

I don't know why so many of us compare ourselves with other women, although I agree it's entirely unhelpful. Particularly when we're comparing apples with lies and airbrushing.

'So stop buying magazines,' goes the next argument. Well, some women don't want to. There are some nice things about magazines – features and interviews and stuff to make and do and buy. Sure, we can steer clear of the mags that make us feel bad and try to limit our exposure to fake female imagery elsewhere, but it's virtually impossible if you want to consume media and pop culture, which I, for one, absolutely do.

What's the answer? Is it for celebrities to start being more honest when asked about their looks? For everyone to photoshop a bit less and then declare it when they do? I think it's all of those things. And I think we need to keep agitating for them. I also think we need to educate ourselves and our daughters about digital enhancement and how the media and advertising industries play with our eyes and minds. Because Cindy Crawford may look smoking hot, but she didn't get that way with an eye cream and some sunscreen.

The Sex Gap

Every time a man lies in bed pretending not to hear a crying baby, a female libido fairy dies. I read this somewhere and I've never forgotten it *because it's true*. They're delicate little things those female libido fairies. Easily killed. Unlike male libido fairies who wear Superman costumes. They are bulletproof and live forever.

For example, men rarely feel too fat to have sex. Men rarely feel too *anything* to have sex. A survey about sex and body image once revealed that 25 per cent of women won't have sex if they feel bad about their body, but only 5 per cent of men would turn down sex for the same reason.

'My wife is sexy and beautiful,' one man said in that survey. 'But she's constantly complaining that she feels too fat to sleep with me and there's nothing I can say to convince her otherwise.'

A woman in the same survey had the reverse problem: 'My husband weighs 198 kilograms. The only sex position he can do is lying on his back. I've tried to tell him that it's hard on his health – not just our sex life. He tells me he's happy and if I'm not, I should find a new man.'

I think we can agree that body confidence doesn't usually impede the male sex drive. Because as hard as I try, I can't imagine a conversation like this:

Woman: [snaking her hand along Man's hip as he reads a car magazine in bed] Babe?

Man: [edging ever so slightly towards the edge of the bed and sighing deeply] Oh, honey, not tonight. I've had so many client lunches this week and I'm just feeling really, you know, beer gutty. Can't we just spoon?'

Yes, okay, I know men wanting sex all the time is a generalisation. I'm sure there are many men who have depression or back pain or just couldn't be bothered.

Sometimes it's the woman who ventures the hopeful hand under the doona towards an unresponsive partner.

'Getting knocked back is even more unpleasant when you're female,' laments one friend, who in her previous relationship was the Not-Tonight-Honey one but whose current boyfriend takes antidepressants that slam his libido. Being on the other side of 'The Hand' has been a shock to her, 'because not only are you sexually frustrated but you both feel like failures. I feel like a rampant sex addict and he feels emasculated. At least with the cliché of the man wanting it and the woman having a headache, you're walking a well-trodden path through millions of marital beds since the beginning of time.'

But for every guy who'd pass up a leg-over in order to roll over and sleep, there are a hundred who'll give it a shot. As one male friend puts it: 'Now that I'm thirty-eight with two kids, saying no to sex would have to mean I was near death and suffering from a broken penis.'

But gentlemen, why wait for an invitation? Why not just initiate sex more often? Go on! You know your wives and girlfriends want it all the time! All the time! There's no such thing as an inopportune moment to try and get jiggy with us! Hell no!

Like when we're sick. We women love having sex when we're sick! Flu, migraine, ebola – any illness is a turn-on!

My friend Angela's boyfriend understands this. That's why he initiated sex with her the first night she came back from hospital. She'd been admitted three days earlier with an agonising bladder infection, caused by – say it with me – having sex. So *of course* more sex was what she'd want when she got home. He was wise to guess that. Although he needn't have waited so long. She would've been fully up for a quickie in the shared bathroom in her public hospital ward.

Angela's boyfriend is not the only one who knows that women want sex all the time under every circumstance. Oh no. Thankfully, there are many more like him. John, for example.

John is married to someone else I know and has cleverly unearthed a secret: women are simply gagging to have sex as soon as possible after giving birth. It doesn't matter if the birth was via caesarean or vagina. Stitches? Pah! It's never too soon to go back for more action. Hell, how great would it be to get pregnant again *before you even left the maternity ward*?

'He actually wanted to have sex in hospital four days after I had our first child,' recalls John's wife, blinking quickly as if trying to process the idea several years later. 'I was still hooked up to an intravenous drip! He did promise to be quick and quiet. And I don't even think he was joking.'

It's not just childbirth and our own illnesses that turn us on. We're also particularly horny when our children are sick. There's nothing like getting up to administer Panadol and clean up vomit at 3 a.m, then stumbling back to bed for a fabulous quickie before the next round of 'Mu-um, I think I'm gonna be sick again!' echoes down the hall.

Yet another terrific time for sex is when we're asleep. It's a rare and selfish woman who doesn't enjoy being woken up for sex. Sleep is for wussbags. The Hand that creeps over to our side of the bed just as we're falling off to sleep or, better still, when we're deeply unconscious will always be welcomed with open arms and legs.

Seriously, though, how much sex is enough? Well, it depends who you ask. Especially in a long-term relationship where there is almost always a disparity between supply and demand. A sex gap.

Here's how you work out the size of this gap. First, establish how many times each partner wants sex per week. Now subtract the lower number from the higher one and that's your sex gap. He wants it seven times a week, she'd be happy with twice? The sex gap in that relationship is five. The smaller the number, the happier the couple, sexually speaking. Zero is the jackpot.

There are many things that can affect the size of a sex gap but biology is probably the biggest. Just like cockroaches can survive a nuclear explosion, so too the male urge for sex can transcend any situation bar actual death. Hung-over? He still wants it. Acute food poisoning coming out both ends? Still wants it. Bedridden with flu and a raging fever? Still wants it. Haven't slept for three months, lost your job, moved interstate and your house just burnt to the ground? Still. Wants. It.

Just been in a lawn-mower accident and missing a limb? 'Never mind my bloody stump, baby, let's go!'

But women? Our libido fairies are easily snuffed out by fatigue, stress, resentment and feeling fat. Oh, and dis-traction. Also known as the wandering mind, this is when thoughts unrelated to the task at hand keep popping into your head and then jumping around like monkeys who have just eaten a hundred red frogs.

This is a common occurrence when you're trying to med-itate and, for women, also during sex.

Or is it just me?

I asked a group of girlfriends about this over dinner one night and everyone reassured me that the wandering mind was extremely common during sex. Sometimes it takes discipline to keep your eyes on the prize, we agreed. 'My boyfriend would be mortified to know what I think about during sex,' volunteered one friend as we got stuck into pre-dinner sourdough and a cheeky sauvignon. 'Last night, for example, we were in the middle of things, but while he was having a blast I found myself wondering what I should wear to work today. I had this client presentation, you see. So he's in the throes of passion and I'm mentally going through my wardrobe, trying to decide if I can wear my brown open-toed shoes with my black pants, which may or may not still be at the drycleaners. And if they're clean and the open-toed shoes look okay, will I still have time in the morning to chop up some fruit for my breakfast? Mmmm, sexy.'

Not very. And yet not uncommon. 'The other night, I'd been reading some gossip magazine before we had sex and I found it really hard to change my focus,' volunteered another friend as the waitress re-filled our glasses while nod-ding. 'At one point my partner asked me what I was thinking about – clearly wanting me to say something hot – and the truth is that I was thinking about what a dickhead Charlie

Sheen is. And not in a sexual way. It's not that I wasn't having fun. I just find it hard to concentrate sometimes. Before I know it, I'm thinking about whether I remembered to give the cat her worming medicine this month, and is soy milk really bad for me?'

It's funny how your sex conversations with your girlfriends change as you get older.

Gentlemen? Don't let *Sex and the City* fool you. Yes, women talk to each other about sex but only as one of an infinite number of discussion topics. And under the umbrella of 'sex conversations' there are many sub-categories, including body image, sleep, contraception, pregnancy and celebrities. Not so much the in–out, graphic details.

'I definitely talk about sex with my closest girlfriends,' one friend admitted, 'but it's restricted to a) am I having it? and b) is it any good? The drunker we are, the more freeflowing the conversation. Only my best friend and I talk in depth about positions and so on. But even that took years to happen and I would never have had the confidence to do that when I was younger.'

For men, the amount they talk about sex is often a measure of how they feel about who they're sleeping with. 'My boyfriend says he and his mates talk about one-nighters or flings but never, ever talk about girlfriends,' confirms a friend who goes out with a surfer. 'Totally off limits. And when a girl starts off as "fun", the best way to tell she's become "serious" is when a guy suddenly becomes prudish about the topic of her and sex.'

If only everyone took a similar approach. Just like there can be a gap around wanting sex, there can also be a gap around how much you're prepared to discuss it. There are some people who insist on regaling everyone with details about their sex life whether you're interested or not. And I'm not.

'I'm hung like a hamster!' declared a man I once sat next to at a dinner party. 'My poor wife is a saint for putting up with me all these years.'

Blessedly, this information was not just for me. It was shared with the entire table during a conversation about Speedos and the pitfalls of wearing them in public. I'm not sure if he was joking, because at that point I turned to the person on my other side faster than you can say, 'Please be quiet or I may vomit.'

It's one thing to confide details to people you know intimately but entirely another to subject strangers to information they're not prepared for.

I once went to a party where two of the guests were a lesbian couple who had recently got together. To say they were fairly into each other would be a bit like saying the sun was a little warm. As they pashed and groped each other throughout the sit-down dinner and practically dry-humped on the dance floor, the other guests were captivated by the show. Just in case anyone was in doubt about their physical attraction and sexual compatibility, one of the women confided to me that they just couldn't stop having sex. 'She sat on my face for eight hours the other day,' she told me. Really? Didn't you, like, put your neck out? Or have to go to work? 'Oh no, it was fantastic.'

I can almost understand it when a relationship is new. Going at it like bunnies and being so palpably high on sexual chemistry can play some havoc with your small-talk radar. But I'm perplexed by those who insist on sharing details of the sex inside their marriage.

Take this frightening encounter relayed to me by a traumatised girlfriend. 'I was at a school function chatting to one of the other mothers I've met maybe three times in my life. Out of the blue she announces she has cystitis because she and her husband had been having so much sex. Cue awkward fake smile and a desperate attempt to change the subject. "Cranberry juice is good," I stammered. Somehow the conversation kept going and she asked me if I'd ever had anal sex. Before I could even mumble, "Oh, bottoms aren't really my thing," she answered her own question saying, "My husband and I have tried it . . . but only about half a dozen times." I managed to extricate myself and head across the room, only to find myself right beside the husband! He must have wondered why I couldn't look him in the eye.'

My friend then went on to explain how the husband was really unattractive. She theorises that some people talk about their sex life to justify their relationship. So the unspoken premise of the sex disclosure is 'my husband may be ugly but he's a tiger in the bedroom'.

Then there's the idea that people talk about their sex life in a bid to elicit similar information from others. And then calibrate themselves accordingly. 'I always wonder if I'm the only one who isn't having sex with my wife,' admitted one guy. 'So after a few drinks I sometimes broach the subject looking for reassurance.'

The opposite of this is sex bragging, particularly popular among young single blokes. For some insight into this, I asked a 25-year-old guy how sex is discussed in his world.

'I've noticed many of my mates who talk constantly about their sex life do it because the rest of their lives is shit. They struggle to come up with conversation to impress and sex is the best they can do. But the blokes who'd have the wildest stories? You never hear a peep from them. It's far cooler to have people wondering what you get up to than actually filling them in on the details. Personally, I never bring up the subject, not because I find it embarrassing but because it's a bit like your parents' sex life – the idea of my friends having sex is too gross. Maybe that's because I'm not a footy player.' Cue raucous laughter.

Whether they vocalise it or not, the average male thinks about sex thirteen times a day, according to researchers – a total of 4745 times every year.

In comparison, women think about sex just five times a day – or 1825 times a year.

That still sounds like rather a lot to me. Unless of course we're talking about a woman whose partner is asking her for sex thirteen times a day and she's saying, 'Are you serious? I'm late for work.' Does that count as 'thinking about sex'?

The same researchers also found one in three guys thinks a candlelit dinner is the best way of getting a woman in the mood, followed by a relaxing massage. Ah, this confirms my suspicions about every man who has ever offered to give me a massage. *I knew it!*

But even if a guy has magic massage fingers and can channel Jamie Oliver in the kitchen, it's not a done deal that every woman will swoon willingly into his bed. There's a growing group of single women who are keeping their legs firmly crossed due to something called the Six-Month Rule. The main principle of this rule is breathtakingly simple: *when you meet a guy you like, don't sleep with him for six months.*

Unlike its retro '90s cousin, the Rules, where women were advised to channel their inner prissy virgin, Six-Month girls are not prudes. Or manipulators. Nor are they necessarily busting to be brides. The Six-Month Rule is not aimed at hooking, trapping or luring a man for marriage, sport or any other purpose. Neither is it some religious movement to discourage pre-marital sex.

According to those who swear by it, the Six-Month Rule is simply a way to avoid dud relationships and protect yourself from unwanted emotional baggage and sexual regret. An added bonus is that it minimises the number of jerks walking around who have seen you naked.

Newly converted Six-Month-girl Sandra is thirty-four and no prude. 'I have no hang-ups about sex and I've slept with more than a few new guys very early on. I thought it was empowering. My body, my decision, blah, blah. It's not like I was hanging out for a ring or even a relationship particularly. But in my twenties, I found myself in a continuous series of short flings with idiots. It took me years to realise that sleeping with a virtual stranger didn't make me feel empowered. It made me feel exposed. Not to mention the way it warped my character judgement afterwards.'

'The day after I've slept with a new guy, I feel great,' echoes Carla, another Six-Monther. 'But even when we both agreed it was "just sex", a few days later I start feeling like crap. Vulnerable and empty . . . kind of wishing I could delete the whole thing.'

Do you have an ex (or five) that you'd cross the street to avoid? Even if it meant walking into oncoming traffic? Now consider how soon into that relationship you slept together. First night? Second date?

Getting to know someone takes more than a date. More than a week. Nerves, alcohol and two people trying very hard to be scintillating can easily be confused with love-at-first-sight chemistry. It's only after spending time with someone in different situations, at different times of day and in different degrees of sobriety that truth surfaces.

Even if the person is perfectly nice, a relationship may not be viable. Or desirable. But if you've already done the deed, this may not dawn on you until waaaay down the track. And here's why: if you're female, sex can interfere with your brain chemistry.

This is called the we've-had-sex-so-it-must-be-love response. Carla can relate: 'I've had so many stupid relationships that should have just been one-night stands. But somehow the idea of casual sex feels slutty, so I subconsciously try to turn it into something more to make myself feel better. Of course, it never works out and I end up wishing I'd pressed eject at the kissing part instead of inviting someone I barely knew into my home, my head and my body. Now that I'm waiting a few months before getting my gear off, I feel more in control. The process of getting to know someone without sex is more fun, more sexy (there's a lot you can do with your clothes on – remember being a teenager?) and more likely to result in either a solid relationship or a nice friendship without bitterness or embarrassment.'

My hippy friend, Josh, explains it like this: 'Exchanging bodily fluids – even with a condom – has an undeniable impact on your energy. You take on some of that person's energy by being intimate. It's especially true for women, for obvious reasons. If you think about all the people you've slept with and all that energy you're carrying around from them, you can see why it pays to think more carefully before exposing yourself to all that baggage.'

In other words, waiting until you know someone before getting busy is the emotional equivalent of using a condom. Safe sex for your psyche.

It's also worth noting that sex doesn't always mean intimacy. It's often hard to pinpoint when a relationship becomes truly intimate. Everyone has different benchmarks. The first sleepover? The first 'I love you'? Or the first time you ask him to buy your tampons? Super.

I once had a conversation about this with a girlfriend whose newish relationship was stalled at the sex stage. Her choice. 'He wants me to stay the night,' she declared to me dramatically with no small amount of angst. Okaaaaay. And that would be a problem because . . . you're an insomniac? 'No, I'm not. I sleep fine.' You don't want to have sex with him? 'No! You know full well that we've been sleeping together for more than a month and it's sensational.'

This was true. I did know all those things because over coffee and banana bread one afternoon in those first giddy weeks, she'd regaled me with many, many details of their horizontal folk dancing. I knew they were doing it with great enthusiasm and had been since their second date. But afterwards, my friend would always retrieve her clothes from his bedroom floor and scurry home to her own bed. Control freak? Commitment phobe? It was unclear, even to her.

Now he wanted to crank things up a notch with some sleeping spoons and overnight cuddles. Maybe a morning quickie before work. Many women would be cheering. So what on earth was the problem with a sleepover between consenting adults?

'It's just too intimate,' she shrugged. More intimate than all the things you've described to me involving various parts of the house and your bodies? 'Yes! Absolutely! Sex is just physical but sleeping with someone – actually sleeping and then waking up together – that's intimate because you're vulnerable. I don't think I'm ready to let my guard down like that yet.'

Working on the basis that intimacy is a key ingredient of a successful relationship, it's interesting to discover how different people define it. For my sleep-shy friend, sex is not intimacy. But for others, it is. 'The first time I have sex with someone is a sign of extreme intimacy,' muses another friend, who is in her forties and single after a series of long-term relationships. 'It's not just about being naked, although that does take courage these days. Having sex with someone you care about – and who hopefully cares about you – is exposing emotionally. That said, I'm not sure the level of intimacy reached on a one-night stand sex is the same level as that reached when you have sex with someone you've been dating and know and have feelings for. And then the next stage of intimacy for me is the first "I love you."'

'Saying "I love you" is my intimacy benchmark,' concurs a 38-year-old male friend via email. 'When I was younger, I'd often trade on the L word to get sex. But from my mid-twenties, when sex was a given by date three and you didn't have to work so hard for it, that word would more often stay in my back pocket. In fact I reckon I've only said it and truly meant it twice in my life.'

It would be tempting to generalise that intimacy means sex for women and love for men, but it's not that easy to split down gender lines. 'Nope, you can have sex or say I love you with no real intimacy at all,' insists another male friend when I float the I-love-you-as-intimacy-indicator theory. 'Intimacy in a relationship is when you're not afraid to let someone see the un-sexy stuff. When a girlfriend can ask me to pick up some tampons from the chemist and we can have a frank conversation about super versus regular, well, that's pretty intimate. Not leaving the room to fart could be an indicator too.'

Damn, I wish I was *his* girlfriend. It sounds so great. Who needs I love you when you can have a companionable fart as a sign of commitment?

Back to my friend who was freaked out by the sleepover. A few weeks after our conversation, she was still feeling uncomfortable about staying the night so she decided to talk about it. With her therapist. 'She said that true intimacy is when we start revealing the parts of ourselves we don't like and saying, "This is me; these are my needs, desires and fears." That's apparently when a relationship truly becomes something deeper.'

After thinking about that for a while, she decided to bite the bullet and spend the night. 'I slept so badly,' she told me afterwards. 'I just couldn't relax.' A few similar nights of bad sleep made her look at the relationship more closely and she slowly realised it wasn't right. The sex certainly felt right, but after four months even that was beginning to lose some lustre. They eventually broke up. The moral of the story? I have no idea. So I asked my friend what she took away from the experience. 'Sex isn't the same as intimacy,' she replied, after thinking it over for a couple of days. 'You can physically have sex with almost anyone, and even if the chemistry is good, it doesn't automatically assume things can progress to that next level.'

Now, if only she'd waited six months . . .

Men Are Different.
They Really Are

I like looking at breasts. Not my own, you understand. My own I mostly ignore, apart from buying them bras. It's other women's breasts I find interesting . . . in a platonic way. I don't get a sexual thrill from looking at them. No, for me it's more an appreciation of form. Aesthetics. Like looking at a nice view. Or a flower. Or Oscars frocks.

There's also the compare-and-contrast thing. I'm forever fascinated by the way women come in so many shapes and cup sizes. And nipples? Well, they're a whole other conversation we'll save for a different book. So many variations, so little time.

That's why I'm not much interested in mere cleavage, or even bosoms in bikinis. Boring. The way they hang, without support, is a crucial part of what makes boobs interesting, don't you think? That's why I prefer to see them nude.

I should probably clarify a few points at this juncture.

First of all, and for the record, I would not buy one of those sad magazines with photos of nude celebrities that are sold in plastic bags. Absolutely not. Wrong context. Too sexual.

Nor would I visit one of those websites that tell you exactly where in a DVD your favourite actress appears topless. Too sleazy and also I couldn't be bothered. I'd never Google 'Julia Robert's boobs' because . . . I just wouldn't. And I rarely take much notice of my friends' boobs except to tell them they look great in whatever they're wearing.

But a topless girl at the beach? I'll always look. Model boobs bobbing along under a sheer top on the catwalk? A terrific opportunity to play my favourite fashion-show game: Silicone? Saline? Or just Seventeen-And-Naturally-Perky?

Of course, the most fun boobs to look at are the famous ones that find their way online via an arty shoot in a glossy magazine. Like Lara Bingle's.

After an old shoot she'd done for a men's magazine popped up on the website of German *GQ*, Australian traffic crashed their server for two weeks. Before that happened though, I'd been one of those who had gazed upon the Bingle Boobies. Then, crash.

A male friend called me a few days later. 'They're gone, Lara's boobs,' he sighed dejectedly.

'Really? That's a shame,' I replied, pretending to care, 'Oh well.'

'What were they like?' he inquired.

'Oh, they were, you know, nice.'

This wasn't enough information for him apparently. Not nearly enough. 'Nice, like, how?' he persisted. 'Perky? Big?'

At this point I had to pause and search my brain for breast adjectives. I don't think I'd ever verbally described another woman's breasts before. Without being able to use my hands as a visual aid, it was surprisingly difficult. Bravely, I gave it my best shot. 'Well, they were big, yes, and full and, um, nipples. And natural. Definitely natural. Very lovely.'

In transcript, this reads like some kind of perverted, smutty phone-sex conversation, but my tone was closer to a real-estate agent describing a sunny studio apartment to a potential tenant. I'd like to think my friend's interest was just as innocuous but it so wasn't.

As a woman, you really can get away with so many things when it comes to other women's boobs. When I worked in magazines, surrounded by women, it was not unusual for someone to interrupt a discussion about, say, coverlines, with a pithy observation such as, 'Jesus, your boobs look good today. New bra?'

And once, I was sitting in a make-up chair before going on TV, chatting to the make-up artist who always did my face, when I commented on how good her boobs looked. 'One hundred per cent unnatural,' she replied. Without thinking, I reached out and gave one of them a squeeze. I'd never felt a real fake boob before. It was very firm. Oops.

'God, sorry, that's probably inappropriate,' I apologised quickly.

'Oh, don't worry about it,' she said cheerfully, instead of charging me with sexual harassment. That could have been awkward.

Not that this would probably stand up in court but my interest in her fake boobs was purely aesthetic, not sexual. And this is fundamental to the way women so often view other women, the key to understanding the difference between girl-hot and guy-hot. Consider this: is it better for a woman to look good in clothes or look good naked? Most women would pick clothes. Most men would pick naked. And this is a crucial distinction.

Women like to check out, judge and comment on the hotness of other women even more than men do. We prefer women on the covers of our magazines and we like to look at women in music videos, on the catwalk, the red carpet and the beach. We have strong opinions about who we think is hot, and often they vary wildly from the opinions of men.

If you've ever had the following conversation with someone of the opposite sex, you'll know what I'm talking about:

Man: 'Wow, she's hot.'
Woman: 'What? Her?! Really? I don't get it. She's pretty but she's not sexy.'
Man: 'What do you mean she's not sexy? She's a babe!'

And so on.

Some men mistakenly believe our inability to agree with their hotness indicator is due to jealousy. Oh no. Please. Lots of women are perfectly happy to hand you a list of women they think are hot and discuss it at length.

Invariably though, our lists leave men scratching their heads. My friend Amanda has a theory about that. 'When girls are rating another girl's sexiness, we add up a whole spectrum of things to equal hot: clothes, style, hair, make-up, career, personality, relationship, lifestyle etc. For boys, it's chiefly aesthetic. It stems back to their biological predisposition to admire all things nubile, fertile, fleshy and come-hithery.'

Fair point. Women don't tend to take fertility or come-hitheryness into account when we're judging hot, subconsciously or otherwise.

Another girlfriend explains it more bluntly. 'The female celebrities I rate as sexy show some class, stay married for more than ten minutes, release only one wedding shot and one baby shot, stand for something, work for a living and don't have a bodyguard carrying their Prada bags from the store. My husband admires girls who look good naked or at the very least wear bikinis while squatting on the cover of a men's mag. Any wonder we don't agree?'

Something else men and women don't agree on is the size of the female bum. Generally, we think our bums are too big and they insist our bums are not.

Unless they're lying.

'Your bum looks big in that,' volunteered the world's bravest man to his girlfriend. 'Huge, in fact.' She was wearing skinny jeans and even though she wasn't a big girl, he was actually right. Brave and right. Because here's a reality check for women everywhere: skinny, ankle-gripping jeans make most bums and legs look bigger than they actually are, okay? They do. So if you insist on wearing them and yet still want your bum to look small, it's unreasonable to expect your partner to hop on the denial train with you.

Fashion is frequently unflattering and a few courageous men are fighting back and calling it like it is.

Jumpsuits? Bubble skirts? Pinafores? Sack dresses? Clumpy mental institution shoes? Kaftans? We think we're on trend. They think we're on drugs.

Ask a woman who she dresses for and she'll probably reply 'myself'. If she's fashionable and honest, she may admit 'other women'. But either way, the subtext is that men are clueless and irrelevant when it comes to judging women's clothes. And that male fashion opinions reside in their trousers, i.e. guys would like us all to dress like Julia Roberts in the hooker scenes in *Pretty Woman* (remember those thigh-high black PVC boots with the micro-minidress slashed at the midriff?). Rubbish, I say.

For fifteen years, I worked exclusively with women. Fearless women in fashion's front row, quite literally. But ever since I fled magazines, I've slowly begun to see women's clothes through the eyes of men.

Here's what I noticed early on: men generally know what looks good on women. Often, they know better than women themselves because they're not influenced by celebrities or labels or magazines. Or other women.

Take the empire line. This is a top or dress that is tight around the bust and then drops loosely. Women love empire lines because we think they look feminine and we don't have to suck in our stomachs. All men hate empire lines for one reason: maternity wear.

When I worked at Channel Nine, one of my responsibilities somehow became overseeing the hair, make-up and wardrobe departments. This was hell for so many reasons, not least because I became the messenger between the male executives and the female fashion department. And back again.

One day, one of the male execs called me into his office. 'Mia, can you have a look at this?' he asked, gesturing to one of his TVs which was playing one of the shows he looked after.

On the screen was a smiley host standing on set wearing an empire-line dress in a bright print. She looked great.

'Is she pregnant?' he asked me, his face creased with confusion.

'Um, no, I don't think so, but I can see why you might ask that.' It was true. She did look great, but on TV, empire line can look an awful lot like maternity.

At the time, it was a huge trend so I was forced to pop down to the wardrobe department and have a word with the stylists. 'Can we have a ban on empire lines?' I asked pleasantly. 'It's making the blokes nervous and it doesn't look great on camera.'

Naturally, this found its way into the media and was reported as: 'Mia Freedman bans pregnancy look at Channel Nine', with some crock about me thinking pregnant women shouldn't be on TV. Right.

To be fair, it's certainly not just TV executives who don't understand the empire-line trend.

'Oh, I hate that!' agreed one guy I asked. 'It's that awful pregnancy look. There's nothing wrong with being pregnant, but if you're not, what's the point of looking like you are?'

My friend Margie discovered this the hard way. 'I'd found the most amazing dress. It was silk, empire line and three times what I could afford, so I knew it was perfect. Got home, tried it on, walked out and Gary said, "Are you joking? You look six months pregnant." I tried to convince him that I did, in fact, look good, and that all men think empire lines look maternity, so he changed his story to, "Okay, you look really fat then." Since I've asked him if I look fat at least twice a day for the past seven years and the answer has always been no, I had to believe him. So the dress was exchanged for an iPod and we were both much happier.'

And this from another friend about another trend: 'My husband Peter doesn't get the way I dress in layers. He thinks I can't decide which items to wear so I just throw them all on at once. I was wearing a strappy camisole over a polo-neck skivvy on the weekend – he thought I'd accidentally put them on in the wrong order and had meant to put the camisole under the skivvy. He looked baffled when I told him my look was intentional and ironic. He said it was actually moronic.'

One friend's partner has an innovative approach to dealing with her fashion train wrecks. A few minutes before they walk out the door he calmly asks, 'Are you going to change before we go?', which sends her into an instant wardrobe crisis. Because look, men may not be fluent in fashion but they're highly conversant in what's flattering. And that's a far more valuable skill.

Quite simply, men like to see the lines of a woman's body. It doesn't have to be skin-tight but they like to know what's under there in broad terms. 'You women spend so much time obsessing about your bodies and not eating dessert,' harrumphs one guy I know. 'I don't get why you then go and wear these kaftany things like Demis Roussos. What's that about?'

That's about being fashionable. And fashionable and flattering live in different hemispheres. Fashionable is bubble hems, pants tucked into cowboy boots, peasant skirts, skinny jeans, tulip skirts (who decided it would be a good idea if women looked like tulips?), Victorian blouses and ugg boots with dresses. Flattering is working your assets to their best advantage regardless of what's on a celebrity or a red carpet.

I know all this in theory and yet I am one of many women who suffer from fashion blindness – the inability to see that the cool look that rocked on Kate Moss actually makes me look like an obese midget. Or a cross-dressing troll. Or simply a try-hard loser. The fact it has a Stella McCartney label does not ameliorate its troll factor.

So why do so many women dress to flatter their fashion egos instead of their bodies? Why are there millions of dollars worth of ugly, unflattering clothes currently hanging in women's wardrobes around this great nation?

Possibly because we scorn the male fashion opinion and then hold an emotional gun to their heads until they tell us we look great. And thin. Does anyone win in that twisted transaction? Retailers.

I do feel sorry for men sometimes. Because when we're not bullying them to rhapsodise over how small our bums look, we're trying to slap confusing labels on them.

First men are told that women want them to be SNAGs and they should cry and emote a lot. Then they start emoting and crying and women decide, 'Oh, that's a bit wet and confronting and could you please harden the fuck up?'

A few years of respite and then someone invents the word Metrosexual. Straight men are suddenly urged to embrace their inner-gay along with waxing and foil highlights. Women briefly warm to the idea of shopping with heterosexual guys but change their minds quickly when they realise his 'n' hers manicures are not sexy. Nor arc straight men with waxed eyebrows. Or a wardrobe of fragrances.

Next comes the Retrosexual and a return to old-school machismo. Blokes are ordered to discard all that Metro namby-pamby nonsense and just be cavemen again. Beer is good. Deep and meaningfuls are no longer necessary. And meat and three veg is as gourmet as you need to get.

Add to this all the hybrid labels like MetroHetero (straights who are 'just gay enough') and MetroGay (gays who are 'straight enough' to be attractive to women) and it's time to break out the neck braces because we all have whiplash.

The most recent label being tossed around, however, is finally one that most men will be keen to get their manly hands on.

It's the Ubersexual. And it's not just the suggestion of extreme virility that makes this word so appealing. This is the Gold Logie label of the male gender.

In her book, *The Future of Men*, author Marian Salzman (who brought Metrosexuals to the masses in 2003), defines Ubersexuals as: '*the most attractive (not just physically), most dynamic, and most compelling men of their generations. They are supremely confident (without being obnoxious), masculine, stylish, and committed to uncompromising quality in all areas of life.*'

But wait. There's more. '*He is passionate about his interests, passionate in his relationships and passionate about doing and being what comes naturally, what feels right, rather than what others believe he should do or be.*'

Ubersexuals shun the out-dated, Aussie male stereo-types of disrespect towards women, emotional retardation, blithe ignorance of anything cultural outside sport, beer and boobs. Ubersexuals embrace the positive qualities of their 'M-ness' (this is apparently the new buzzword for masculinity although I don't quite understand what was wrong with the old word for masculinity but anyway . . .).

His best friends are male. He loves and respects women but doesn't consider them his 'buddies'. He dresses for himself, isn't interested in fads and doesn't shop for entertainment.

The descriptor 'uber' was chosen because it means 'the best, the greatest', says Salzman. Indeed. Try reading out some of the above descriptions to any bloke within a 50-metre radius and watch him write, 'I'm an UBERSEX-UAL!!' on a Post-it note and stick it on his forehead.

This is very different to the word Metrosexual, which made men nervous. It also made women nervous, to be honest. The extremes of straight male behaviour – Retro and Metro – may be interesting to read about, but in real life no woman ever wanted to put all her relationship eggs in either of those baskets.

According to Salzman, the media and advertising industry

are so busy portraying men as womanisers, wankers, wusses or woefully clueless that they've overlooked a significant shift in the real world. Either by accident or by design, Ubersexuals have cherry-picked all the best, most attractive qualities of men from the past several decades and integrated them into a modern, sexy package. Young men are very well represented among Ubersexuals but Ubers span all generations.

America's largest ad agency, JWT, recently published a list of the Top 10 Ubersexuals, which included George Clooney and Bill Clinton. There ain't no cloud over the sexuality of these guys. No man-bags being carried here.

The King of the Ubersexuals? The guy they judged best embodied the essence of all things Uber? Bono. Rock God. Charity crusader. Father. Husband. Sexy. Smart. The ultimate Uber. I bet he has great sperm.

In the space of a month a little while ago, I learnt three new things about sperm. Firstly, sperm travels at a speed of 42 kilometres per hour. I'm not sure if this is inside or outside the body but it's pretty darn impressive. Who knew those little buggers were so fast?

The second thing I learned is that some men are extremely paranoid about women stealing their sperm, speedy or not.

And the third is that other men are extremely keen to give their sperm away.

But let's kick off with the paranoid guys because, gee, they're fairly committed to their belief that there's a rampant group of sperm stealers out there masquerading as – wait for it – women who want to have sex with them. Why? So that they can get knocked up and then steal all his money, of course!

And how are they dealing with this irrational fear? By ripping off their undies and running to the doctor for a pre-emptive vasectomy in their twenties and thirties. Believe it – there's a growing trend for young single American men to undergo the snip to protect their precious DNA.

As with most modern trends, this one appeared to start with a celebrity. In 2006, American football player Tom Brady broke up with his girlfriend, actress Bridget Moynahan. Soon after, she announced she was pregnant with his child and he announced he was dating supermodel Gisele Bündchen. An obscenely good-looking mess ensued, played out in the tabloids, naturally.

Some cynical blokes perceived this situation as an example of 'man-trapping' (girl meets boy, girl 'tricks' boy into getting her pregnant, girl extracts eighteen years' worth of child support out of boy). But according to US men's mag *Details*, man-trapping is now called 'oopsing'. As in 'Oops! That must have been a Tic Tac I swallowed, not my birth-control pill!'

I'm sure this does occasionally happen but often? Often enough to make you so suspicious of women that you'll willingly have surgery on your testicles and forego the prospect of ever becoming a father? Some snip-happy men say, 'Yes, cut me, Doc, and cut me now.'

'Now I can never have a girl say I made her pregnant,' 23-year-old college student Marcus Whitlock bragged to *Details* magazine after pretending to a doctor he was thirty, forking out $850 and limping happily away after a fifteen-minute vasectomy. 'I don't have to worry about being tricked.'

The magazine also unearthed Tim Vass, 'a 34-year-old from Florida, who got snipped after a half-dozen pregnancy scares, including what he says were two attempted Oopsings. Both of the latter were one-night stands; he says one woman admitted she didn't know who the father was and the other demanded a DNA test that proved her wrong.' Now that the safety of his sperm has been secured, Tim reckons sex is 'like eating junk food and knowing you're not going to get fat'.

Excuse me, gentlemen, but have you heard of condoms?

Less expensive. Less painful. Less permanent. Less risk of contracting an STD. Oh wait, too late. You're already neutered. Oops.

At the other end of the sperm spectrum are the guys who are super keen to give their DNA away. And they *want* it to be used specifically for making a baby.

A single girlfriend of mine was about to turn forty and was desperate to have a baby. I suggested she consider a sperm bank. She did.

After selecting a suitable donor online, she began the process of trying to fall pregnant. During this time, she was totally open about what she was doing, sharing her news with anyone who asked. 'I've got nothing to hide or be ashamed of,' she reasoned. 'When I'm pregnant, everyone's going to find out anyway. And it's quite the conversation starter.'

The reaction was overwhelmingly positive. In fact, from many men it was a little too positive. 'As soon as they hear I'm using donor sperm, they fall out of their pants with eagerness to offer me theirs,' she marvelled. Even though she didn't ask for it and doesn't want it.

'First it was my ex-husband who offered, then my ex-boyfriend. This was bizarre because neither of them was interested in having children with me when we were together and both of them are now married with kids of their own. Go figure. Then, a friend's husband volunteered *his* sperm. Now my neighbour – also married with a kid – has offered to be my baby daddy. When will it stop?'

My friend politely and repeatedly explained that she wanted an anonymous donor so she would not be tied to someone she wasn't in a relationship with. But still, they persisted with their offers as though competing in some kind of Sperm Idol contest. She continued to receive texts like this: 'I'm clean!' And this: 'I've talked with a lawyer and it's easy!' And this: 'I really want to help you, let's discuss it more.'

Thanks but no, she replied to each of them. No, no, no. And also? No.

So much sperm. So little interest in using it.

And still the offers kept, er, coming. But why were they so keen? Was it some primal competitive urge to spread their DNA? Was it because my friend wanted no emotional attachment? Was it an ego thing? Or were the sperm pushers just being altruistic?

Sometimes scuffles over sperm break out in long-term relationships. Even marriages. Especially marriages.

In the past few years, I've become fascinated with the

following question: when it comes to having babies, how do you know when you're done? When is it time to put the sperm and eggs out to pasture?

One friend answered my question like this: 'Today, I'm not done. My three-year-old slept the entire night, dressed herself this morning, ate a good breakfast and didn't howl when I dropped her at kindy. But on other days, she tries to crawl into my bed four times during the night, then in the morning she refuses to get dressed, eats no breakfast, demands rainbow Paddle Pops and ends up being dropped at kindy in her pyjamas looking like something DoCS should investigate. On those mornings? I'm done.'

A male friend discovered the answer at a charity dinner when his wife put her hand up to bid for a vasectomy.

Oddly, when you have a baby, one of the first things people ask is when you're going to have another one. This is often before your internal stitches have dissolved. And it never stops. Mums of young children frequently ask this question of each other, often as a way to sort out their own plans and feelings. I know I do. Just like single women will often ask married women, 'How do you *know* when you meet the One?' I'm constantly asking other mothers, 'But how do you *know* when you're done?'

For many, the question is not one of choice. Nature or circumstance may decide how many – if any – kids you have. But if the choice is yours, where do you draw the procreation line?

Is it a financial decision? 'We want to send our kids to a private secondary school and two lots of school fees will already be stretching us to breaking point,' one father of two told me.

A practical one? 'I couldn't bear to buy a people mover and we'd like the kids to have their own rooms,' said a mother of three.

An emotional one? 'We're already so stressed with our full-on jobs and juggling the needs of one child,' admitted the parents of a five-year-old. 'The three of us are a happy little unit. Adding another baby would spread us too thin.'

For some, it's a question of gender. 'If our second had been another boy, I would have gone again to try for a girl,' admitted one mother of two. 'But having one of each . . . I was happy to stop. Although my husband would have liked at least one more.'

When one partner is done before the other, it can be problematic. Hence the sperm scuffles. A few years ago, when a mate told me his wife was pregnant again, I was surprised. When we'd spoken about it before, they'd said their two children were enough. She'd wanted more but he said no way. So when I heard the news about number three, I asked him what changed. 'I like having sex with my wife,' he shrugged. 'She went on strike until I agreed to bin the condoms.' Ah, never say never.

'At my six-week check-up after having my daughter, my parting words to my obstetrician were, "I hope I never see you again as long as I live,"' remembers one friend who had a very bad birth. 'But you forget the pain and the horror, don't you? And there I was back in his office again two years later, pregnant with my son.'

One way to make sure you put a full stop after your last child is to go for the snip. I know half a dozen dads who have trotted off for a vasectomy in the past couple of years, all willingly.

'Oh, we're so done – the kitchen is most definitely closed,' laughed the wife of one of these men. 'Not only is it closed, the electricity has been disconnected and the appliances removed.'

A few months after having my daughter, I was standing in a deli, bouncing her on my hip while waiting for a chicken schnitzel roll. 'Is she your first?' asked the guy behind the counter. 'No,' I replied, trying to shut down further inquiries.

But my new sandwich-making friend wanted more info. 'Your second?'

Pause. 'Um, yes,' I mumbled reluctantly. Pause. Wait for it. I knew what was coming.

'So are you going to have a third?' he asked.

As I pondered my answer to this big question, the other customers pricked up their ears to hear if I'd be getting knocked up again any time soon.

I decided that the best form of defence was attack. 'What about you?' I countered. 'Kids?'

He beamed, delighted with the opportunity to discuss it. 'My wife is due next month with our first.'

'How many would you like?'

'I'd like five but she only wants two.'

'Maybe compromise on three and cross fingers for twins.' I suggested to murmurs of agreement from the sandwich crowd. His kitchen wasn't closing any time soon.

All the Single Ladies

The evening was not going well and it was my fault. I'd arranged to meet a single girlfriend for dinner and we'd had the usual lengthy email negotiations about where to go. My friend pointed out that since it happened to be Valentine's Day, getting a table anywhere would be a complete nightmare.

Naturally, I dismissed her concerns with an airy 'Oh, we'll be fine', convinced, as I often am, that if I'm not interested in something (like celebrating the cheesiest day of the year with a romantic dinner), then no one else is likely to be either. I've always had the unshakeable belief that a romantic gesture made on 14 February counts for far less than the same gesture made on any other day due to the sheep-like pressure to perform. It's commercial and tacky and unoriginal.

Doesn't everyone feel that way? It certainly didn't seem like it when I turned up at the restaurant I'd suggested.

Astonishingly (only to me), it had been transformed from a cool, laid-back bar into a candle-lit sea of tables for two.

I was late and my friend was early – an ugly combination. She'd been sitting at the bar tensely sipping a glass of pinot for twenty-five minutes before I arrived and she was not happy. With me.

'Hi!' she greeted me aggressively, the clear sub-text being 'you-are-a-complete-dick-for-suggesting-this-place-and-I-hate-you'. Hmmmm, I was a little taken aback at her hostility. Yes, I'd stuffed up by ignoring her suggestion to make a booking, but surely that wasn't a hanging offence? Tonight it was.

'I've been sitting here by myself, feeling like a bloody *hooker*,' she hissed.

'Oh, honey, you don't look like a hooker!' I reassured her brightly. 'You look lovely! That dress is so —'

'I do *not* look lovely,' she hissed. 'I look like a tragic loser waiting at a bar on the most couple-y night of the year. See that table of single women in their fifties all dressed in black? They're having an alternative Valentine's celebration and just asked if I'd like to join them *because I looked lonely*. And that group of sleazy men over there with wedding rings? They offered to buy me a drink *to cheer me up*. Can we leave now please? I want to die.'

As she stomped towards the door, I trailed apologetically in her wake and tried to work out what the hell had happened. My friend was no victim. Nor had I ever seen her bitter about being single. After an amicable divorce two years previously and turning forty in December, she was a poster girl for modern single life. She was successful at work and loved her own company. She had several men chasing her, dated when she felt like it and was in no hurry to find the next One. No chip on those shoulders. So what had triggered this meltdown?

Two things. Well, three. As we wandered the street looking for Plan B, I listened as she unpacked some surprising emotional baggage. 'Every woman at work got flowers today,' she blurted.

'Red roses with baby's breath?' I snorted. 'That's so lame!'

'Easy for you to say when you're married,' she shot back.

I carefully reminded her she'd been married and it hadn't made her happy.

'If I'd been in a relationship, I wouldn't have even wanted flowers. But that's not the point. I felt like a freak. As if everyone were casting a critical eye over my single life, and marking it "INADEQUATE" with a fat red Texta.'

I remembered reading once that to show empathy you must listen intently and then paraphrase the person's feelings back to them to prove you understand their pain. 'You mean, you felt like Jennifer Aniston when Brad and Angelina got together and had a million rainbow babies?' I paraphrased eagerly. 'Or the other members of NSYNC every time Justin Timberlake picked up a Grammy?' She was scowling now but I was on a roll. 'You felt left out? Foolish? Humiliated?' She shot me a look of death.

Okaaaaay. Back to silent empathy and supportive nodding.

'And my sister got engaged last week.' Ah. No need for celebrity analogies or paraphrasing here. It's always confronting when someone close to you takes a step down a path you've diverted from. 'Ah,' I repeated out loud.

'Of course I'm excited for her, but when everyone's coupling up, sometimes it's hard to be perky about paying every bill on your own. Am I being a wuss by secretly wishing I had someone to share the load with me?'

I pointed out that sharing the mortgage didn't make her happy in her marriage. And if there was financial pressure, she could look at re-financing. 'Oh, stop doing that male thing and being logical and trying to *solve*,' she exploded. 'Just let me vent, *okay*?'

That's me back in my box then.

When we finally found somewhere to eat that only had an hour's wait for a table, the mood lifted a little. The capri-oskas helped. So did the book about photography I'd found for her on Amazon as a late birthday gift. Well, at least she didn't throw it at me because it was a hardback.

'You know what I think really pushed me over the edge, today?' she said, as our dinner plates were being cleared, her anger dissipated by laughter and a wagyu beef burger. 'I left my mobile at home.' Um, yes . . . and . . .? 'It's been years since I sat alone at a bar without being able to text or call someone and look busy. I felt pathetic just sitting there with my wine. Conspicuous.'

I got it. Sometimes the littlest things can trigger an emotional avalanche. In a sea of lovey-doveyness, it turned out my friend didn't need the crutch of a ring or a rose, just her iPhone.

***

If Valentine's Day is a difficult one in which to be out and about when you're single, weddings are worse.

Not because of bitterness or jealousy. But because there is no other occasion on earth when your relationship status will come under such scrutiny. Forget a suit or a floaty Lisa Ho frock. If you're an unmarried wedding guest over thirty, you may as well wear a sandwichboard emblazoned with the words: 'PLEASE ASK ME WHY I'M NOT MARRIED YET!'

One time at a wedding reception, I bumped into the bride's sister, Lara, hiding in the bathroom. It was almost time for the bouquet toss and she was desperate to escape that peculiar indignity of being rounded up like cattle with the other single girls to compete for a wilting bunch of peach and white roses.

I knew Lara quite well so we didn't have to wade through much of the usual wedding small talk ('Beautiful bride!' 'Stunning dress!' 'Terrific speech!') before she abandoned the niceties and started bitching. 'When will this be over?' she muttered darkly into her champagne. 'I just want to get the hell out of here.'

Lara was single and about to cry, but these two things weren't connected in the way you might think. You see, she was perfectly happy being unmarried. At thirty-four, she'd just bought her own flat, was kicking all sorts of goals at work and had a great life filled with travel and friends and job satisfaction.

But all of this was irrelevant to the relatives and friends of her parents who could only see – and comment on – her naked ring finger. 'I was feeling fine about my life before I got here,' she ranted, reaching for my champagne now that hers was gone. 'I was happy! But all anyone wants to know is why I'm still single. After a full day of it, I just want to drag my sad old spinster ass home and stick my head in the oven. If one more bloody person asks me, "So, Lara, when will it be your turn? Anyone special in your life?" I'm going to beat them to death with a bonbonniere.'

What made the whole thing even more bizarre was that this was the bride's second wedding in three years. She'd split from her first husband less than a year into that marriage and had instantly rebounded into the arms of a high-school boyfriend. But no one mentioned how strange it was that the bride had boomeranged back to the altar so fast. No, no, no. The Abnormal Freak Prize was unanimously awarded to Lara for being – gasp – unmarried at thirty-four.

'Oh, don't worry, it will happen for you one day, dear,' yet another old aunty soothed, patting her hand before adding a cautionary warning: 'But don't leave it too late!'

Too late for what is unclear. Perhaps she will turn into a pumpkin. Or shrivel up and blow away. Is it better to grab the closest available man and cling for dear life even if you're incompatible and the marriage disintegrates? Well, yes. A failed marriage – heck, even two! – seems to make some people less uncomfortable than no marriage at all.

I don't believe the same affliction affects single men at weddings. There is no Spinster Syndrome equivalent. Regardless of age, unmarried men are not made to feel like they've failed. Their single status is seen as their choice and even their triumph. They're rarely the objects of pity or concern. More like a wink and a nod at their unspoken virility and roguishness. Very George Clooney, yes?

You're unlikely to find anyone resembling George Clooney at the horror that is the singles' table. Every wedding has one. In my single past, I remember once being seated between the bride's socially dysfunctional forty-year-old cousin and the groom's lecherous divorced boss. I spent most of the wedding hiding in the toilet and feeling like meat. Single meat. At least I was seated with adults. One girlfriend was appalled to discover she'd been placed at the kids' table at a family wedding. She was twenty-eight. Her tablemates were aged eight to fourteen. She had a terrific time. Oh, wait.

Singles aren't the only ones doing it tough at weddings of course. Unmarried couples are in a special hell of their own. 'It was horrendous and I was totally unprepared,' cringes a mate who took his live-in girlfriend to a wedding last year. 'The subject of marriage had come up a couple of times in our relationship, but we'd agreed that for now we were happy and why rush it.'

At least he thought they'd agreed until the twenty-seventh time someone at the wedding asked, 'So what are you two waiting for?' and his girlfriend's forced smile became a bit wobbly. They ended the night with a huge row in the cab home. 'She wanted to know what exactly I *was* waiting for, and we had to have one of those really long "Where is this relationship going?" talks. She said she felt humiliated and I said I felt claustrophobic, like I had a marriage gun to my head.'

Oh, yes, nothing like a wedding to shine a klieg light on your relationship! It's the elephant perched excruciatingly on the lap of every unmarried couple in the room.

Of course, not all weddings are ghastly for single guests.

Occasionally, the singles' table bears fruit. 'It's definitely a good place to pick up,' notes one happy bachelor who's had many a sleepover with a fellow wedding guest. 'Girls seem to get all mushy and lower their guard. Maybe it's an unconscious desire to mate and head towards their own big day.'

Funnily enough, he's not yet married any of these girls. 'Don't worry,' I console him, 'it will happen for you too one day. Just don't leave it too late, okay?'

Even for a married couple at a wedding, all that optimism and love buzz emanating from the bride and groom can trigger some pretty interesting conversations.

A few years ago I went to an incredible wedding. It was a biggie, probably the largest I've ever been to, with hundreds of people and a 10-metre-high wall of roses. But of all the extravagant details, it's the groom's speech I remember most vividly.

When speaking about his new bride, he observed that in most relationships there is a Giver and a Taker. 'I'm a Giver myself,' he noted, 'and so is Michelle. In the past, we've each always gone out with Takers.' The newlyweds locked eyes at that point and grinned at each other before he continued. 'I can't tell you how wonderful it is to be in a relationship where there are two Givers. It's a revelation for us both and I highly recommend it.'

It did sound pretty great, all that mutual giving. A Give-Fest. Imagine that. As the groom wrapped up his speech, I noticed a few elbows jabbing into ribs among the married guests at our table.

The rest of the evening was a revelation of a different kind as verbal skirmishes broke out between couples determined to establish who was the Taker and who was the Giver. There was much jockeying for position.

'I'm *so* the Giver,' I heard one woman insist to her husband as we passed them on the dance floor. 'Yeah, totally,' he replied while rolling his eyes. 'You give to yourself.' And then she hit him. Affectionately. I think.

With some couples, the starring role of Taker and the less flashy, supporting role of Giver are very clearly defined. From the outside, anyway. Think about the couples you know. And it's fair to say those roles don't necessarily remain static. Over time, they can ebb and flow, influenced by a million external factors like kids, work, stress, money and health. Sometimes you just don't have much to give. Sometimes your tank is empty.

Also, it would be a mistake – and a stereotype – to

assume that women are always the Givers and men the Takers. Not so. I know plenty of female Takers and many men who are extremely nurturing. In a healthy relationship, I think it all balances out over time.

However, the idea of some people being inherently and consistently a Giver or a Taker is an interesting one. And it doesn't just apply to couples and relationships. It can apply to friendships too.

I consider myself to be a pretty nurturing person. I've been fortunate enough to have had some generous mentors in my career, and perhaps that's why I've tried to maintain that same philosophy across all areas of my life. Well, except for the times when I'm too busy being a needy and demanding Taker to give a sausage. It happens.

Still, it's always a surprise when I encounter people who just Take. All the time. Unflinchingly. Or, as my friend Wendy puts it: 'Some people have a "receive" button but no "send".' And she's right, you know. Spot on, in fact. Extreme Takers are a mental and emotional drain on your time, your energy and ultimately your patience. Know any?

These are the people who will sit at dinner or on the phone and talk about themselves incessantly. Extreme

Takers will hijack your ears with their problems and barely make a token enquiry about your life or wellbeing. They are a giant pain in the ass but they can be rather difficult to eradicate from your life, because if you are a Giver, they will gravitate towards you and suck up everything you have.

Am I sounding bitter? Oh. Really? Why yes, I have indeed clocked a couple of these people in my life over the years and I have given them chance after chance to dig deep and find that receive button. Repeatedly, I have been disappointed. In my experience, Extreme Takers tend not to change.

On the most basic level, this taking and giving begins with small talk. There's an unspoken understanding in female conversation called the Rule of Small Talk. It's very simple really. You must seek information, and then offer it. You talk. You listen. You take turns. There are some men who find this confusing, and many a first date has come a cropper when a woman asks a man questions as per the Rule Of Small Talk, but while answering her questions, he becomes swept up in the subject matter and finds himself on a roll. 'This is great!' he thinks. 'She's so interested in me and what I have to say! I must say more about me and then she'll be even more interested!'

Except no. Wrong. You crossed that invisible line where

you forgot to 'give' the other person a turn in the conversation because you were too busy taking all the oxygen in the room for yourself. No second date for you, buddy, let alone a glowing wedding speech.

Of course remembering to ask as well as answer questions on a date is only one part of an extremely complex and mysterious recipe for success. In those fragile early stages of meeting someone and deciding to get to know them a little better, some things are just unacceptable.

Some things are *so* unacceptable that when someone does them in your presence, you suddenly don't want to have sex with them, even if you were considering it a moment ago. Like wearing Crocs out to dinner. Or being rude to waiters. Or living with your parents past the age of thirty. Or kissing badly. Or using the word 'panties'.

On a date, these things are called Dealbreakers. In a relationship, they're just called Things-About-You-That-Piss-Me-Off, although the no-sex outcome is often the same.

Dating Dealbreakers are the invisible little lines we have in our heads that, when crossed, make the person who crossed them instantly unappealing. Sometimes we don't even know a particular line exists until it's crossed. And, alas, then it's too late.

Dating Dealbreakers are responsible for many new relationships not getting past the first or second date mark. This is the time Dealbreakers usually rear their heads, when the ecosystem is so delicate that the slightest thing can cause irreparable damage.

Person One innocently does something that grates on Person Two so severely that Person Two immediately decides they can never see Person One again. Instantly, sex is off the table.

Sadly, Person Two is almost always blind to the fact they've committed a Dealbreaker and Person One will rarely be honest enough to tell them. So Person Two is forced to blunder on through the dating wilderness until he or she happens upon someone with entirely different Dealbreakers. Someone who isn't bothered by the way Person Two answers their mobile during dinner. Or that they wax their chest. Or have a monobrow. Or snort when they laugh.

Dating Dealbreakers are not necessarily rational. Nor are they always fair. And they are highly individual. What may be intolerable to one person may be no big deal – or even appealing – to another.

'If a guy wears shoes without socks, I'm outta there,' shudders one girlfriend. 'I have a thing about cutlery,' rants another. 'It kills it for me when a guy holds his fork in his right hand like a spear and his knife in his left.' 'Too much fake tan,' says a guy friend. 'It stinks and all I can think about is how it will stain my sheets if we have sex.'

I once went on a date with a lovely guy I met through work. The chemistry wasn't quite electric but we had a nice time. Dinner and a movie. At the end of the night I let him kiss me, more out of sympathy and boredom than actually wanting to. Still, I probably would've agreed to another date were it not for the first words that came out of his mouth afterwards. 'Oh, what a lovely French kiss.' That was it for me. Deal broken.

But my favourite story ever belongs to a friend who unwittingly committed a Dealbreaker on her first date with a guy she'd met online. They'd had great rapport over email and the phone and he suggested meeting on his boat one Sunday afternoon. Dressed in jeans, sandals and a nice shirt, she met him at the marina. It turned out he actually lived on the boat, even though it was extremely small and had no shower. He kept telling her he was very successful – a banker or something – and explained that when the weather was bad, he slept in his office. Fine. She had an open mind. A bit odd but whatever.

Sadly, the chemistry didn't translate in person, and after a pleasant afternoon she made her excuses and went home.

The next day, she received the following email.

Nicole,

Sorry. I wasn't a very good date yesterday. It wasn't very chivalrous of me.

I am just always disappointed on a first date when a woman shows up wearing pants. I realise there's probably not a message being sent, but it's a flaw of mine that I think there is. I believe I'm being told that I'm not worth the effort. Sometimes, when I see a woman in a dress out with a man, I look at him and wonder what makes him better than me.

I have always felt that the woman that I'm going to marry will be wearing women's clothing when we first meet.

I'm actually thinking about putting in my online profile something along the lines of 'please consider wearing a skirt on our first date'.

Actually, I wonder why women wear dresses to their weddings if they are against wearing them on dates. This seems inconsistent. A first date is a prerequisite for a wedding, isn't it?

Anyway, you are an attractive, articulate woman and whoever is with you is fortunate. Take care.

Aaron

After my friend had picked up her jaw from her keyboard and had forwarded his email to all her friends, she sent Aaron the following reply.

Dear Aaron,

I appreciate your honesty and I thought I should be honest in response. All my life I've dreamed of my wedding day and wearing my fantasy bridal outfit . . . white jeans encrusted with crystals. After reading your email, it seems I may have to reconsider my dream.

Sometimes I see a man walking down the street with a woman in jeans and I can't understand what's the matter with me . . . Why can't I get someone like him? Am I not worthy? I hadn't thought of a first date being the prerequisite for a wedding, but I suppose you are right and I will take this newfound knowledge with me as I search for my future denim-tolerant husband.

Kindly,

Nicky

Wow. When trying to set up single friends, I've never thought to ask for wardrobe preferences. Perhaps if I did, I might have a higher strike rate.

I am quite possibly the world's worst matchmaker. I lack subtlety, empathy and finesse. I'm impatient and demanding. I have no attention to detail. In short, I'm what Bridget Jones identified as a Smug Married who has totally forgotten what it's like to be single. My background assumption is always: 'You're both single! There you go! You're welcome!'

Take the following conversation I had with a guy whom I set up with one of my girlfriends. With signature restraint, I called him at 8 a.m. the morning after their blind date.

Me: 'So . . .? How did it go?'

Him: [awkward] 'Um, well, she was nice.'

Me: [annoyed already] 'What do you MEAN "nice"?'

Him: [clearing throat] 'Well, she's . . . nice but I just don't think we have much in common. '

Me: [pissed off now] 'But you have lots in common! You're both . . . single. And you're both in your thirties and you both know me. There! Three things in common at least!'

Several months earlier, after setting up a girlfriend with a different guy I knew, I found myself saying this: 'I really think you should keep an open mind about him. Persevere! Just because you didn't find him attractive . . . I mean, chemistry doesn't have to be there from the start necessarily! Once you get to know someone, it can develop and you can suddenly find yourself wanting to have sex! You can! Go on! He's such a great guy!'

The subtext to both these conversations was something like this:

Them: 'Sorry, nice try but I'm just not that into him/her.'
Me: 'Don't be so selfish and picky, dammit! No wonder you're single.'

Rationally, I understand this is wrong, unfair and unrealistic. My expectations are always stupidly high. When I set up two people I like, I expect them to have instant chemistry, fall rapidly in love and then, at their wedding, make a heartfelt toast of gratitude to me that inspires a standing ovation. That's all.

Slight problem though. So far, my attempted matches have never led to a second date let alone sex or commitment.

Heck, I don't think I've even managed to orchestrate a drunken pash between two horny singles. That's how rubbish I am.

My inadequacies were highlighted one time when I watched a true pro at work. We both know this terrific man who is divorced and looking for a serious relationship. When an old friend of mine came out to Australia for an extended holiday, the matchmaking pro and I agreed we should set them up. I stood back in awe and took notes as she worked diligently.

The difference between us? My modus operandi is to hurriedly hype one person to the other, gloss over any unpleasant historical details and negative character traits and stay very big-picture positive. Vague and embellished. Enthusiastic and pushy.

But the pro, who has several successful matches (including one marriage) and whose own marriage was the result of a set-up, takes the opposite approach.

She says the key to matchmaking is to put thought into it. It's not brain surgery but it requires serious attention to detail. Like identifying things they might have in common (beyond my criteria of, say, both living on earth and breathing oxygen) and making sure they have complementary or compatible personalities. *Before* you introduce them. Who knew?

She also believes it's vital to give each party a very detailed brief about the other including a recent photo. 'Don't leave anything out,' she insists.

Ignoring much of her advice because I am lazy, I now do my set-ups over email. I don't think you can even call it matchmaking. It's more a quick intro and get the hell out of there.

But I can't shake the feeling of frustration when it doesn't work out. If I like two people, why on earth wouldn't they like each other? Let me count the ways.

Yes, yes, I know, dating is a difficult, mucky business. I do understand this, even though I haven't been on a date for quite some time due to marriage. After years of hanging out with old farty couples, suddenly a bunch of my friends are newly single and reporting back from the frontline, so I'm armed with all sorts of fresh intelligence.

And the news is surprising. Besides technology and the advent of the cougar, not much about dating has changed since I was single. It's still awkward and exhilarating and frustrating and nerve-wracking and perplexing all at once.

I was not a natural at dating. Never liked it much. At one memorable point, I was forced to implement a 'no alcohol' rule for first dates. This is because the purpose of a date is to discover if you have chemistry with someone. And after a few drinks? You have chemistry with everyone. Even the waitress. Even the waitress's dog. Everybody is witty and sexy, especially you. And this is a problem. All that faux chemistry can make for some confusing false starts with people who should never have made it past 'Thanks, nice to meet you. I'm hailing a cab now.'

At a birthday party my daughter went to recently, I got chatting to one of the other mothers called Jo, who was recently divorced after a twelve-year marriage. She was thirty-eight and her two sons had stayed at their dad's the previous night while she'd gone out with a group of friends to a bar. There, she'd drunk too much red wine and a 22-year-old had flirted with her outrageously. I learnt all this in less than sixty seconds because women are highly efficient at exchanging personal information. What began as small talk, soon turned into a fascinating insight into what it's like to be a newly single adult in modern times.

In short, dating has changed. It's all messed up. No one dates within their own generation any more. Gen Y and

Gen X date each other, and sometimes the age gap between partners can stretch to twenty years. Or even more. But somehow, it works.

Having not been single for yonks, I had many questions for Jo. 'What's it like out there?' I began, grabbing a passing pink cupcake. 'Oh, you have no idea,' she said from behind very dark glasses. 'It's mental. Insane.' The next half an hour flew by as she verbally downloaded Dating 2.0 into my hungry ears.

I added this intelligence to the information I'd already gleaned from some newly separated and divorced friends who were staggering dazed and confused around a singles landscape they no longer recognised. May the force be with you if you suddenly become single again after a long bout of coupledom because you will not understand who you're meant to date or who wants to date you. So. Until they make GPS for navigating the single scene, some of the following information may be useful . . .

If you're a single woman in your thirties or forties, you must forget about dating men your own age or older. They do not want to date you, not even a little bit. They will be looking over your shoulder at a party, scanning the room for twenty-something girls. This is because they think you are too much hard work and you have too much baggage. Twenty-somethings carry teeny tiny bags, as a rule. And they rarely have children in them.

The single men in their thirties and forties are either committed bachelors who fancy themselves as George Clooney or, if newly single, are looking for nothing more than a good time. Now that they're no longer bound by the constraints of a relationship with an equal, they're looking for inequality – mentally, emotionally and physically. On their shopping list? Simple. Young. Sexy. Adoring. Easily impressed. No kids.

This usually changes after some months or years, but in the early stages of singledom it's all they want.

Happily, they find it in the twenty-something women who share their disinterest in hooking up with anyone their own age. These girls are looking for a partner with experience. Direction. A car. A career. A wallet.

None of this is surprising. Older-man-dates-younger-woman is hardly a newsflash. What's interesting is the way the dynamic has shifted among the two remaining groups: twenty-something guys and the newly single women in their thirties and forties.

There's been so much written about the denigrating cougar phenomenon that casts older women as preying upon the fresh meat of younger men. But what do you call the twenty-something guys who enthusiastically pursue older women? Do they have a name? They need one. Because there are lots of them and the women they're trying to pick up are rather bemused by their ardent attention.

Like Jo. 'I can't believe how full on these young guys are,' she marvelled to me back at the birthday party as the hired fairy amused the kids. 'They start flirting and at first you just assume they're drunk or the lighting is bad and they can't see how old you are. But even when you reveal your age, they're not in the least bit fazed. Even if you're fifteen or twenty years older! Even when you mention your kids!'

At this point we were joined by another single mum who nodded her head vigorously. 'Me too!' she exclaimed. 'It's the strangest thing! I keep thinking I can put them off and escape by mentioning the fact I'm a forty-year-old single mother but it just seems to make them keener. I never thought I'd be with a younger guy but the ones my age aren't interested, so if you want sex or a boyfriend, there's not much choice. I guess there are worse things than sleeping with someone who has a great body and thinks you're fantastic. Oh God, I sound like my ex-husband – he's forty-one and dating a 23-year-old PR girl.'

When I was in my early twenties, I didn't know any guys my age who dated older women. So what changed?

From the frontline, Jo floated her theory. Newly single mothers aren't looking for a commitment. They've done marriage and kids. They need a rest and some fun, not happily ever after. Twenty-something men are looking for the same thing. 'They have no sense of consequences or the future, which makes them incredibly confident,' she marvelled. 'The idea of an experienced woman who has her shit together is appealing. Also, the older divorced guys usually have kids themselves so they don't want the hassle of someone else's. Bizarrely, it all works out and everyone is happy.'

Well, unless you want to make pop-culture references your partner will understand. 'The only time I'm reminded of the eight-year gap is when we look at each others' iPods,' laughs one of my friends who's with a younger guy. 'I've not heard of any of his bands and he thinks Madonna and Coldplay are lame and tragic. He'd never heard of Culture Club!'

Not knowing who Boy George was had not proved much of an obstacle to my friend's love. Because she was, indeed, in BIG LOVE with her new boyfriend who had only been on the scene a few months.

And while I was happy for her . . . well, you start saying very predictable things when you've been in a relationship for a long time. Especially when you're talking to people who are newly IN LOVE. Note the caps lock. In this case, it doesn't mean shouting. It means INTENSITY. The kind of INTENSITY you feel when you are newly IN LOVE.

This feeling is called infatuation, and although it may feel intoxicating, it often leads to trouble because you don't make good decisions in this state. Instead, you make spectacularly dumb ones.

Author Elizabeth Gilbert wrote about that in her book *Committed*, the follow-up to *Eat, Pray, Love*. The title refers to marriage rather than mental illness, although in the infatuation chapter the two sort of collide.

Reading it, I learned that the brain scans and mood swings of a cocaine addict are startlingly similar to those of an infatuated lover. Yes, infatuation is an addiction complete with chemical effects on the brain, measurable by scientists. And just like a junkie, an infatuated person is blind to their future welfare. Physical and emotional risks? No problem. Whatever it takes. Love is the drug and they need some more.

According to Gilbert's research, infatuation is most potent in a relationship's first six months, with anthropologists noting that many babies are conceived during this time (oops etc.). So possibly infatuation is nature's way of keeping us sexually reckless enough to ensure the survival of the species.

In the past year, a handful of my friends have begun new relationships. Bright, shiny, new relationships that make them EXTREMELY HAPPY.

This is a marvellous thing, although it can be a little disconcerting to eat at restaurants with people who pash between courses and think they can put their hands up each other's clothes without anyone noticing. I noticed.

Anyway, I'm genuinely happy for my friends and their hands and all their other happy parts. So why do I find myself trying not to frown as they giggle about not having spent a single night apart since they hooked up? Why do I silently 'tsk-tsk' when they excitedly mention moving in together after two months? Or confess to being careless with contraception because 'it just feels so right'?

The problem is that infatuation is often a crock. A mirage. 'A trick of the endocrine system,' according to Gilbert, who points out infatuation isn't the same thing as love. 'It's more like love's shady second cousin who's always borrowing money and can't hold down a job.' (I think I dated that cousin. Yes, I definitely did.)

That's because in those early days what you're actually entranced with is the reflection of *yourself* in the eyes of someone who wants to sleep with you. It's like two blank pages dazzling each other with pristine potential. Only later do you notice all the fine print. Which is a major bummer if you are already pregnant or have matching tattoos.

The other problem with infatuation is speed. Generally, relationships that start fast also end fast. I've learned this the hard way in my own life and watched it happen to others predictably often. Some men have a particular tendency to hit the accelerator early, give themselves whiplash and then fling open the door so they can bolt from the moving vehicle. Neck braces all round.

Privately, when the new lover isn't there, I can give my infatuated friends that worthy little speech about building foundations. 'Take it slow,' I caution, while they nod and smile insincerely. 'If you stay at his house every night, you don't leave any room to ramp things up when you know each other better. It's still early days!'

Despite the nodding and the smiling, I'm aware that my sage counsel is about as welcome as a wisdom tooth extraction. Without drugs.

You know when you're trying to talk some sense into

someone and they pretend to listen but you can see they're just wondering when you'll shut up so they can bolt home and have sex again? It's like that.

There's more. 'Research has also shown that people are far more susceptible to infatuation when they are going through delicate or vulnerable times in their lives,' writes Gilbert. 'The more unsettled and unbalanced we feel, the more quickly and recklessly we are likely to fall in love.'

Ah, holiday romance. Far from home, when everything is unfamiliar, Unsuitable Local Dude can easily be mistaken for Mr He-Completes-Me.

I did this big time when I lived in Italy. Aged nineteen, I dated a sweet guy in Florence, and when the time came to return home to Australia I decided my reluctance to resume my 'real life' and start university was because of him. Love. It must be. Well, infatuation anyway.

So we entered into one of those torturous, ill-conceived long-distance relationships that seem like a terrific idea at the time. Of course it wasn't and the whole thing staggered forward for months, culminating in him arriving in Australia to visit me and me taking one look at him walking towards me in the airport and realising I'd made a horrible mistake. Awkward.

Similarly, if you're going through a rough patch due to illness, relationship problems, work stress or anything else that throws you off balance, you're particularly vulnerable to infatuation. Apparently, this is because when your emotional guard is down, you're more likely to do the duckling thing and imprint on the first creature that crawls past your cracked egg.

I guess that explains why rebound relationships are usually so intense yet doomed, and why most rehab programs recommend recovering addicts avoid new romance for a minimum of twelve months after getting sober. Infatuation.

It may also explain the odd dodgy relationship in your past. You know, the one you look back on and wonder, 'WTF was I thinking?' Chances are you weren't. You were just infatuated.

There are many of my past relationships I look back on with the sobriquet WTF. I'm not sure if infatuation can be blamed for all of them. Some of them defy explanation.

Have you ever dated a loser? Sorry, that's unkind. Let me rephrase the question. Have you ever dated someone who is . . . not quite living their life to its full potential? A bong-head, say? Someone who is immature and irresponsible?

Lost and directionless? Wilfully negligent about their health or personal hygiene? Someone in desperate need of therapy? Someone living with their parents past twenty-five? Someone with a mullet?

Perhaps you need some thinking music while you cast your mind back through your romantic archives. While it's playing, I'll go first and admit to having dated one or *cough* three such individuals in past lives.

Here's the thing: you know how all the self-help books and the relationship gurus preach that *'people never change and what you see is what you get and trying to change someone you love is futile etc., etc.'*?

Well, they lied. There *is* one guaranteed way to make someone change. To force somebody to morph into the best possible version of themself. And it's this: break up with them. Not just briefly or as a warning. Forever. Dump them and move on with your life and they will transform in your wake. They will become fabulous and successful and you will gnash your teeth and become bitter. It's called the Butterfly Effect and if you've ever dated a caterpillar, you may have experienced it.

What is the opposite of Schadenfreude, that feeling of satisfaction that can be derived from someone else's misfortune? Is it Freudenschade? Is that how you describe the resentment you can feel about someone else's success? Oh wait, I think that's called Being A Bitter Cow.

I once dated a guy who was a human bucket of problems. Drank too much, collected bongs, almost unemployed, lived with his dad. A total catch. In my defence, he was very good looking and I was going through a brief and shallow bad-boy phase. When I finally woke up and realised I'd had a gutful of bong stains on my coffee table and holes in my wallet, I walked away, relieved. Of course, this was his cue to turn his life around, move overseas, discover his true calling as an art director, land a prestigious and well-paying job, and hook up with a 22-year-old swimsuit model.

That would be the Butterfly Effect. And years later, I was not remotely bitter when I read about their glossy New York life in a magazine. I felt not at all resentful about the time, money and emotional energy I wasted on him when he was a caterpillar. Oh no, not me. I wish him and his swim-suit wife all the very best.

I have many friends who feel my pain, having wasted months and years on caterpillars of their own. Like Jody (fake name, true story) who lived with a bookkeeping stu-dent in her mid-twenties, a period she refers to as 'the

Forgotten Years' because they were so boring. 'He was a sweet guy but just so dull,' she remembers, frowning. 'I couldn't interest him in travelling anywhere or meeting new people or even trying different foods. He was totally dependent on his mother, who still did all his washing and rang every morning to wake him up. Oh, and he'd always answer the phone, even if we were having sex. That drove me mad.'

Naturally, after Jody fell in love with someone else and ended the relationship, he got his act together. 'He made a career change to movie producing, something he'd always dreamed of doing but never had the guts to pursue even though I encouraged him endlessly. Now he works with some of the world's most famous actors and directors and lives this incredible life. He's happy and successful and lovely and I hate him.'

I know another woman who divorced her husband a few years ago only to watch him become the man she always wanted him to be, inside and out, and marry someone else. 'Why couldn't he have been like that with me?' she often wonders. 'How come *she* gets to benefit from all the years I begged him to go to therapy to sort out his issues? How come *she* gets the bloody butterfly and I got the guy who wore a farting Mambo dog t-shirt with Reefer sandals and used alcohol to block his emotions?'

Then there are the relationships where one person waits patiently for the other to be ready to do something big. Move in together. Get married. Have a baby. Buy a dog. Be monogamous.

Endless angst and arguments fail to resolve the impasse and the relationship ends. Then the one who wasn't ready meets somebody new and suddenly? They're ready. That happened to my friend Nathan. 'For the five years we were married, Sandy said she didn't want kids. In the end, it's what broke us up because I really wanted to start a family. Before we'd even finalised the divorce settlement, she was pregnant to a guy she'd met at work. I was gutted.'

Sometimes, butterflies are a bitch.

Is This Normal?

I've never had sleeping babies. I know not what that is like. As many new mothers do, I have often blamed myself for the fact that my babies don't ever magically sleep through the night of their own accord. Surely I did something wrong. I gave them a dummy. Or I didn't. I breastfed on demand. Or I didn't. I did dream feeds. Or I didn't. Their rooms were too hot or too cold. I ate the wrong food. I had them in my room. Or not. I put them down at the wrong time during the day, letting them sleep too long or not long enough. I let them cry or I went to them too quickly.

There are many, many ways to beat yourself up at 3 a.m. and I was familiar with them all. It's a very lonely time, the middle of the night. Lonely and desperate and maddening.

In those first six months with each of my babies, and for years with my first, sleep did not go well. I would be up to feed and settle anything from three to eight times a night. Every night. And as I sat there, in that wasted state, trying not to fall back to sleep sitting up, I had time to ponder many things apart from my own inadequacies as a mother.

Like whether celebrity new mums were as sleep deprived as regular new mothers. Katie Holmes had her daughter, Suri, within weeks of my daughter's birth and I thought of her rather a lot at 3 a.m. Was she awake with her baby too? Or could she somehow buy herself sleep with nannies and nurses? If she was breastfeeding (which Tom helpfully announced she was; I was eagerly awaiting an update on how her stitches were healing), well, then she'd have to be up, right? You can't out-source your boobs, as appealing as that thought was to me as I battled mastitis again and again.

Sometimes I would look at the clock and it would say 4.20 a.m. and I'd remind myself that there were people in nightclubs dancing on podiums. This always cheered me. Because there's something so lonely about being awake in the middle of the night. Is it the quiet? The dark? Or just the knowledge that everyone else is fast asleep? Except they're not.

It seems no one sleeps well any more. From children wandering into your bed to stress-induced insomnia, from restless leg syndrome to snoring partners . . . as singer Ben Lee observed in one of his songs: awake is the new asleep. Especially at 3 a.m.

That's why sleeping pills are now the drug of choice for the thirty-plus demographic. The same people who used to score illegal pills from dealers to help them stay awake all night now score legal pills from doctors to help them sleep, if not all night, then at least for a few hours. At dinner parties and in office kitchens, the sleep deprived discuss the relative merits of Stilnox versus Normison and the best way to procure them.

You used to have to invent excuses to get a prescription for sleeping pills – if by 'invent excuses' you mean 'tell lies'. Like 'I'm going to Europe and I need to sleep on the flight.' This was always a good one. Simple, clinical and invites no further questions. Unlike 'I can't sleep because I'm stressed/depressed/miserable,' which could lead to aggravating inquiries about your stress levels and suggestions you try meditation, counselling or giving up coffee. But a doctor friend recently told me that lies are no longer required. Doctors are sympathetic to sleepless patients and are probably often sleepless themselves. Stress is now a legitimate reason for a prescription.

Stress has never kept me awake at night. No matter what's going on in my life, even through periods of intense anxiety where my days have been hellish, I've always been able to sleep. Maybe this means I'm shallow. But even good sleepers like me can't escape other causes of sleep disruption such as noisy neighbours and those bloody birds that start singing at 4 a.m. at the start of spring. And kids.

I have a friend whose one-year-old son wakes up at 4.30 a.m. for the month before daylight savings starts. To let the rest of the family sleep, my friend sacrifices his own and takes his son to Bondi each morning to pace the promenade with the pram. Stumbling alongside him in the pre-dawn darkness are at least a hundred other sleep-deprived fathers doing the same thing. (Tangent: I bet these men get lots of sex from their grateful wives.)

Before you have kids, your nights are fairly predictable. You get into bed where you might read or have sex and then you go to sleep. After children, anything is possible after dark. There is no certainty.

One night, when we were away with the kids and renting a holiday house, I had a particular doozy. Exhausted from seven months of getting up a thousand times a night, I heard my son crying, again, and stumbled down the corridor towards the room he was sharing with his sister. With my eyes half closed, I overshot the door to their room and fell down the stairs.

This sounds slightly more dramatic than it was. There were only four stairs but they were made of stone and it hurt. The circus continued. Hearing the loud crashing and louder wailing, my husband Jason leapt out of bed to investigate and was quickly faced with a dilemma. Who should he comfort first: hysterical son in cot or hysterical wife on floor?

This was my daughter's cue to wake up and demand a detailed run-down of the situation. She was followed swiftly by the dog, who was so delighted at this unexpected 2 a.m. family gathering that he ran to get his ball in the hope someone might throw it for him. My eldest son slept through it. Bless him. No matter. The technicolour bruises all over my hips and legs told the story adequately the following day.

If babies aren't waking you, other things still can. Like a neighbour's cat setting off your burglar alarm. Or the toy clock in your kid's showbag inexplicably playing a loud beeping version of the *Lone Ranger* theme at 4 a.m. Or a possum deciding it would be a good idea to have sex in the roof above your bed at 2.45 a.m. A possum on Viagra who goes at it with gusto for two hours.

One morning, I was recovering from a badly broken night while sipping tea and watching my fresh-as-a-daisy friend Lisa Wilkinson interview a doctor about sleep deprivation on *Today*. I was not fresh as a daisy. I was the Loch Ness Monster in Peter Alexander pyjamas with bed-head and a bad attitude.

As the doctor listed the dire consequences of less than six hours' sleep per night – obesity, clogged arteries, heart disease etc. – Lisa blessedly cut him off, exclaiming she'd now be lying awake at night worrying about lying awake at night. See you there.

When Remy, my youngest son, was four months old, two long months before Elizabeth the Sleep Whisperer came and gave him the Gift of Sleep, I had a friend whose baby was two months younger and yet slept through the night. Twelve hours straight. Each time we spoke, I made her describe to me in graphic detail how well rested she felt. What it was like to have hours of unbroken sleep, to go to bed and stay there for hours. *In a row*. Hearing it made me so happy. It was like sleep porn.

Desperation drove me to develop a radical theory about

sleep deprivation at that time and it was this: keep your expectations low. Unspeakably low. Like, if you don't fall down the stairs, it's a good night.

Something else I unearthed, as part of my discovery that there were many unsleeping people just like me, is that there are also many people who don't wake up in their own beds.

And these people are not just singles who got lucky the night before. Even if you're married or living with someone, there's a good chance you didn't wake up beside them.

An epidemic of bed-hopping has swept Australia and it's coming to a house near you. Perhaps it's already there. Perhaps you already play Musical Beds at your place. We do. Because when you have small children – and even when you don't – falling asleep beside your partner doesn't guarantee you'll wake up in the same bed. Or with the same person.

There are three main reasons couples sleep apart:

1. THE DOGHOUSE. This is where you go when you are booted out of the big bed due to some kind of transgression. A night in the relationship sin bin rarely involves an actual doghouse, unless you've been really, really bad or are so drunk it seems like a sensible place to crash. Mostly

'doghouse' is a metaphor for the spare room, the couch or, occasionally, the car.

2. KIDS. When they're small, children have a tendency to require attention during the night. This is a common cause of Musical Beds and goes something like this. House wakes to the sound of crying. Both parents pretend to be asleep, attempting to bluff each other into getting up to deal with it. Regular breathing and absolute stillness is essential. Crying crescendos until Parent One caves, swears loudly and resentfully stumbles out of bed towards source of crying. Parent Two smugly congratulates self on sterling acting job and considers nominating self for Oscar. Meanwhile, Parent One seeks revenge on lazy-ass Parent Two by bringing wailing Child One into marital bed. Soon, Child One is no longer crying but not sleeping either. Child One wriggles and kicks restlessly until Parent Two, no longer smug, is forced to abandon marital bed for relative peace of . . . Child One's now-empty bed. Child Two, woken by swearing and traffic in hall, gets up to investigate. Discovers Parent Two squashed uncomfortably into Child One's small rocket-ship bed with legs hanging off end. Locates missing sibling in big bed with Parent One. Looks fun. Decides to join party. Parent One now shoved to side of big bed and forced to sleep

on mattress piping while Child One and Child Two sprawl like starfish, sleeping soundly.

To meet this challenge head-on, I know one family whose three young kids all have double beds. This way, everyone gets a decent sleep, no matter who ends up crashing where or with whom. 'I haven't woken up next to my husband in a year and a half,' admits the mother. Another mum whose toddler doesn't sleep feels guilty that her husband has to go and sleep in the spare room whenever their toddler shoehorns herself into their double bed. 'I know I should be stricter about the way she ends up in our bed every night but I'm trapped in the sleep-deprivation cycle and it's just easier for one of us to go and sleep somewhere else. Hopefully she'll grow out of it before she gets to high school . . .'

3. LIFESTYLE. Maybe one of you snores. Or comes to bed late and checks their email in bed. Maybe one of you gets up at 5.30 a.m. to go to the gym. Or has insomnia and likes to read. Maybe one of you has hot flushes and wants to sleep with only a sheet. Lifestyle issues like these are causing an increasing number of couples to choose, by mutual agreement, to sleep in separate bedrooms. Some occasionally. Some regularly. Some permanently.

Often, it's an age thing. Sleep gets lighter as you get

older, snoring gets heavier and a spare bedroom may conveniently become available when the kids leave home. One person will be driven into the spare bed by desperation and, once there, discover that sleeping solo is the answer to a good night's sleep.

This is not a new phenomenon. People have been doing it for yonks. But it's always been hush-hush due to the stigma; the mistaken assumption that separate beds must mean doghouse and/or no sex. In fact, many solo-sleeping couples find the opposite is true. 'There's no bigger passion killer than lying awake all night next to a large snoring man,' shudders one woman I know. She's found she's far more likely to want sex after a good night's sleep. 'And when you sleep separately, it's not just the dreaded wandering hand under the doona as you're drifting off. It's actually quite fun to say, "Your room or mine?"'

In a story called 'To Have, Hold & Cherish, Until Bedtime', the *New York Times* recently blew the lid off this dirty little marital secret, declaring separate bedrooms a full-blown global trend.

It seems lots of people don't want to sleep together any more and it has nothing to do with sex. Architects and builders are reporting an avalanche of requests for dual master bedrooms, and a survey by the National Association of Home Builders predicted an astonishing 60 per cent of custom houses would have two main bedrooms by 2015.

Once it was his 'n' hers towels. Then bathrooms. Now bedrooms. What's next? 'A lot of people I know fantasise about living in the same apartment building as their husband – but in a separate apartment,' sociologist Pamela Smock told the newspaper. 'That could be next.'

Living together apart? Almost. There really is a sociological trend towards this and people who do it are called Living Apart Togethers (LATs).

I generally find there are two types of couples: those who start living together on the first date and those who don't. The first group tend to burn through their relationships on speed while loudly gushing things like, 'He stayed over that first night and he just never left!' Until he leaves permanently. Instant co-habitation often ends in broken hearts and broken leases.

Of the second group – those who take their relationships slower and steadier – there's a growing number choosing not to live together. At all. These are the LATs.

In the course of my research, I met Aaron and Amy who

have been together for four years. They are in love and committed. Monogamous. They spend five nights a week in the same bed. But they live apart. They are LATs. She tells me it's more romantic and she relishes her independence. He tells me he enjoys his space and likes missing her when she's not there.

During the time she spends alone at her tiny studio apartment, here's what Amy likes to do: 'I like dressing up for him for dinner, him not knowing what I'll be wearing, getting a chance to go home and fake tan, put on a face mask and be a grot, solo. I might squeeze blackheads or pluck in-grown hairs. I like eating cereal for dinner in bed with my laptop. And I still appreciate all of this, even if it's only for one or two nights a week.'

Here's what Aaron likes to do: 'I spend as long as I want on the toilet with a car magazine. Sometimes I sing while I'm there.'

Julia hasn't lived with a bloke since she ended a five-year de facto relationship at twenty-nine. Now she's thirty-nine, with a handful of long-term relationships behind her – all LATs – and a firm resolve to continue living alone. 'You get to keep the mystery alive,' she exhorts. 'He's not taking a leak while you're shaving your legs. You keep your space.

His friends watch sport at his place, you watch the Oscars with the girls at yours. It means things aren't rushed. You get to keep your finances separate and not argue about money. It stops the irritation levels because those cute, endearing things at the beginning can turn into the ones that shit you when you're sharing an enclosed space 24/7. Living together churns through your romance quota so much more quickly.'

Preserving romance. LATS talk about that a lot when explaining their choice to live apart. And in a back-to-the-future twist, a number of LATs women freely admit they're waiting until they get engaged or married before calling the removalists. 'You've got your whole life to live with someone once you're married, so why rush it?' insists Amy. 'If and when Aaron and I move in together, I want it to be for an exciting, romantic reason, not just because one of our leases expired.'

Other factors prompting committed couples to live apart include burnt fingers (survivors of marriages or de facto situations that ended badly), geography (proximity to work, family) and other complicating factors (kids from previous relationships, finances etc.).

You'll also find eating cereal for dinner and performing unglamorous yet essential beauty rituals in private on the list of Top Reasons Why Chicks Dig Living Alone.

Oh, and wardrobe space.

In a society obsessed with quickly shuffling you onto the next stage of your relationship, LATs can confuse people by refusing to play the what's-next game. 'So when are you moving in together?' everyone asks. 'Never,' they reply contentedly. Because for them, living separately is a positive, grown-up act of choice, not born of commitment phobia or lack of love. They're just happy with the way things are.

But there are challenges. 'You have to be very secure in your relationship to not need that moving-in-together milestone,' admits Julia. 'Some people assume that it means your relationship isn't monogamous or that one of you isn't really committed.'

'For me, not living with a boyfriend is difficult,' admits one friend, who has been a happy LAT for the past two years of her relationship but is flirting with the idea of going de facto. 'The boundaries confuse me. For example – do we talk every day? Are we meeting for dinner tonight? Do we do sloppy nights at home in our trackies or do we always meet out? How long does the dating ritual last? But there are those moments when I'm bleaching my moustache, retrieving ingrown bikini line hairs or having two huge cups of Milo for dinner that I think how suffocating it would be to live with a man.' With a sigh, she imparts the following wisdom: 'Living apart needs courage and patience, and living together seems to need exactly the same . . .'

The best thing about living apart, I think, would be avoiding that peculiar hell called 'combining our furniture'. This rarely goes well. There's a lot to be said for ye olden days when young people moved straight from their family home to their marital one. Do not pass go. Do not collect stray bits of furniture from markets, relatives and IKEA.

At least then your new home would be a blank page on which you could both project your interiors taste, as you discovered what, in fact, it actually was.

But not now. Oh no. These days by the time a couple move in together, they've both got a truckful of assorted bits and pieces they've accumulated since they moved out of home. And invariably, they will hate each other's furniture on sight.

Usually in such situations, the chick wins. Women tend to be the default arbiters of taste when it comes to interior design.

Proving, yet again, that I am abnormal. You see, when God was handing out interior-design genes, I must have been lying on a beach reading a magazine. Clearly, I forgot to join the queue. Because by the time I brushed the sand off me and lined up, it was all over and there was nothing left. What other explanation could there be for my utter disinterest in all things interior? While I can appreciate other people's good taste, I am bamboozled by the world of furniture and finishes. And what even *is* a finish?

Some say that when you're talking to a dog, all it hears is, 'Blah blah blah, FIDO, blah blah blah WALK, blah blah blah DINNER.' I'm like that with interiors. Admittedly, I would rather eat a box of hair than have a conversation about renovations. But if I'm forced to participate, I find it difficult to make sense of the words, or even hear them. 'Blah blah blah CHAIR blah blah blah RUG blah blah FLOORBOARD something blah.'

It's not that I don't *try* to understand; it's just that my brain keeps wandering off to think about what I might like to eat. Or starts composing a witty text to a friend. Or ponders what high school the children should go to. Or whether Stella McCartney had her babies too close together. Sorry, what? Swatch of what? Huh? Is that my phone ringing?

A few years ago, we did a brief spot of renovating. Actually, that's a lie right there. The words 'brief' and 'renovating' are mutually exclusive and should never be allowed in the same sentence. Time has clearly dulled my memory.

Anyway, during this renovation, it's fair to say I was ambivalent to the point of supreme disinterest. I couldn't have cared less. I couldn't have cared less than less.

I left it all to my husband who, fortunately, had a clue and did a sterling job. But one night, desperate for some input from me or possibly just to amuse himself, he insisted I participate. I waved my arm around a bit and said things like, 'Oh, darling, I trust you. Whatever you decide is fine with me. And . . . is that my phone ringing? Goodness, I have to urgently answer it and speak to . . . someone. Anyone at all.'

Despite my desperate attempts to look purposeful and run from the room, he forced me to sit down and cruelly made me look at an array of sample charts and swatch thingies.

'Which of these finishes do you like for the floor in the kitchen?' he demanded.

No idea. None.

'What about this one?'

'Oh, it's okay. I guess. Yep. Sure! Great idea! Can I go now?'

'No. And what do you think of this one?'

'Um, I don't know. Possibly I don't like it as much as the other thing but it's still quite nice.'

'Well, it's leather and those are couch samples. Not great for the floor.'

And then I wandered off to play on my laptop as he fell about laughing at me.

Happily, that was pretty much the last time I was asked to contribute to the renovation process. Which suited me fine. Sure, I had to put my control-freak tendencies on ice, but if that was the price for not having to look at fabric samples and visit furniture shops and make cost comparisons and measure things up and place orders and think endlessly about how this texture might go with that tone and deal with tradesmen and builders, I was delighted to have no say.

However, this hands-off attitude appears to make me a freak. A traitor to my sex. Every other woman on earth was apparently born speaking fluent furniture. Except me. Me no speakie Ottoman.

One time I was at a work function and chatting with some colleagues when the subject of my renovations came up. Clearly, my female colleagues had taken *their* place in God's renovation-gene queue. And then gone back for seconds. They were very keen to ask about my renovation and share tales of their own.

Aware that my eyes were glazing over and I was thinking about dinner again, I interrupted with, 'Oh, I'm not really involved in the details. My husband's doing all that.' For a moment, I thought I might have accidentally said, 'Oh, have I mentioned I'm Hillary Clinton's secret lesbian lover?' That's how shocked they looked.

'Are you SERIOUS?' exclaimed one. 'Wow! That's so . . . brave!' shuddered another, clearly disturbed that I was leaving such crucial decisions to someone without a vagina.

Virtually all my close friends are borderline gurus when it comes to interior design. One is a stylist. Another one may as well be. Their style is innate. But I do have one friend with great taste who wasn't born that way. She married into the world of design; her husband is a talented builder who works in the family business designing, building and furnishing beautiful homes. 'I grew up in the 'burbs where chocolate was a food, not a colour,' she says. 'It was a shock to learn that there were some chocolates that "read" mushroom and some that "throw" lime . . . and oh, by the way, we're talking about carpet!'

Over the past fifteen years she's learnt to speak

interior – and exterior – quite fluently and has grown confident in her own choices. 'You have to make mistakes. Isn't that why eBay was invented? To sell a disaster chair that "reads" purple instead of aubergine . . .'

Naturally, I had no idea what she was talking about. All I caught was 'blah blah blah eBay blah'.

Interior design does seem like rather a social activity. All that talking to people about samples and whatnot. All that driving around to look at things and ask for quotes. Maybe that's another reason I feel exhausted before I've even begun.

These days I have to struggle to go out for fun reasons let alone dull ones.

Whatever happened to my social stamina?

My capacity for socialising has never been sensational. But lately, it's sunk from moderate to laughable. I'm not sure if this is because I'm getting older, I have small children or I'm not single. Possibly all three.

Firstly, the getting older thing. Speaks for itself. As your twenties retreat, comfort elbows excitement off the top of your list of Things I Want From My Saturday Night. And sleep replaces spontaneity as Ingredients Of A Really Good Weekend.

You need at least a week's notice to be spontaneous when you've got kids. That's how long it takes to organise a babysitter. Kids are not conducive to social stamina, mostly because parenting chews up most of your stamina full stop.

And that little bit that's left? Hard to let it roam free and stay for one more drink when the meter is running on the babysitter. Because, you know, that drink will cost you $10, and then it's another $15 for the babysitter, and an extra kilogram of remorse you'll have in the morning when you're hung over and the kids want you to mash their Weet-Bix at 6 a.m.

In many ways, having children is the ultimate social experience because you are never alone. And if you have a daughter, she will never stop talking. Kiss goodbye the sounds of silence for they will be but a distant memory once your girl learns to speak.

My family are among my favourite people to hang out with but they certainly suck up a lot of my social energy. This actually suits me down to the ground but it can be a little annoying for those who want to see me and to whom I did not get married or give birth.

For example, one Saturday a while ago, I found myself on my phone, as I often do, making excuses. Friends had invited us to a barbecue and I didn't want to go.

Well, I *wanted* to go. I like the *idea* of going. I did. But I'd already spent a couple of hours chatting with the other parents on the sidelines of my son's cricket game and I had a girlfriend dropping around for coffee. The next afternoon was my niece's birthday party. And these days that's already far more social activity than I can handle in a single weekend.

'Look, I'm sorry,' I gushed apologetically into my friend's voicemail (Voicemail! High five!), 'but it's just a bit of a full-on weekend and look, I'm going to be honest, I'm just a bit hopeless and really tired and, well, did I say I was sorry? Anyway, have a great night and I'll be thinking of you and I promise I'll be there next time. And, well, sorry. Okay, bye! Sorry!'

The relief I feel after cancelling a social arrangement is palpable once I knock back the bitter shot of guilt. It's like stealing some extra time back from life.

Of course when you're single and actively looking not to be, time alone is not a priority. The hands-down biggest influence on your social stamina is your relationship status. It's this simple: single people have more energy. I think it's primal. When you're single, Mother Nature seems to provide a happy dose of natural amphetamines that help you go to just one more party, have just one more conversation, stay up just one more hour. The longer you're out, the more people you'll meet and the better the chance that one of them will ring your bells. And then it's only a hop, skip and a jump to procreation and – bingo! – the continuation of the species.

As one friend puts it, 'I go home early from parties now I'm married because I've already landed the cutest guy in the room. And he's a sure thing.'

'Single people can stay out longer because going home means another night of being single,' agrees a single friend who was borderline anti-social when she was shacked up but happily went out five nights in a row last week. 'It sounds pathetic, I know, but going out – and staying out – keeps alive the hope of meeting Mr Right or Mr Right-Now. Imagine he turns up just after I leave and some other woman meets him? That's what keeps me from nodding off and stops me from noticing the stinking club full of sweaty people. When I'm in a relationship, all I want to do is nice things with other nice couples in nice places. Or sleep! But now that I'm single again, I have all this energy. I call it single energy. I'm sure it will vanish again when I meet someone.'

A single guy friend describes the vague sense of guilt he

feels about staying home. 'Even when I'm exhausted and can't really be bothered, the motivation kicks in because I feel like single people should be out. I want to meet someone and I'm not going to meet her on my couch. That thought gets me out the door. It's the lure of potential, of possibility.'

Not everyone subscribes to my theory that social stamina relates to age or circumstance. 'Nup, it's something you're born with, like eye colour,' insists the girlfriend whose barbecue I ditched when I discuss it with her afterwards. 'Social stamina is predetermined and then perfected. My partner has endless reserves of it and I've struggled to keep up ever since we met twenty years ago. I see it in our kids too. One loves to play at home in his room and the other needs constant stimulation and activities. It's nature, not nurture.'

Another friend emails me this in response to my question on the subject: 'My nickname has been Cinderella for years – always home before midnight, even in my twenties. I married the Roadrunner (famous for early unannounced departures). We did a runner from our own wedding – ordered a car for 10.30 p.m. and slipped out the back way much to our friends' disgust and our joy.'

Personally, I've made peace with the fact that I am no longer a very social person. Never was, to be honest, even back when I was single and childless. These days, I'll take the lounge room over the bar every time.

Regardless of your social stamina and what you do on them, weekends are always welcome. Everyone loves the weekend. Wait, they don't. Not everyone. Some struggle with it. Others secretly dread it. And yet very few people ever talk about it.

Nicole Kidman and Keith Urban did acknowledge it when they named their daughter Sunday. Asked about the significance of her name, Nicole explained in an interview how she and Keith both used to struggle on Sundays. 'If you're lonely, Sunday is a very lonely day, and if you're happy and you've got your family around you, then Sunday is a beautiful day.'

Word. Weekends can be like birthdays in that they prompt reflection. If something is off, all that unstructured thinking time without the distractions of the week can feel oppressive.

For a creature of routine, weekends can be destabilising and unpredictable. And yes, they can be really, really lonely. They also have a hint of the Christmases about them – you know how you're *meant* to be all jolly and you feel like a freak if you're not? Like that.

Even when you're in a good place and happy with your

lot, weekends can be challenging. Writer and mother of two small children Heather Armstrong once admitted on her blog to dreading weekends: 'I have to brace for hours and hours of moaning and screaming. But then, it's not just the screaming, although that is a big part of it . . . It's hard for me to sit still knowing there are a million projects I could be working on. I can't sit on the couch and read a magazine any more, and it's driving me crazy.'

I am not like Heather in this regard. I *can* easily sit on the couch and read. Any time. Bring it on. It's just that my kids won't let me.

Truth is, my favourite thing to do on weekends is mooch around at home with my family, enjoying their company. Love it. So naturally, I've found a way to feel guilty about this.

The guilt manifests itself as a nagging voice inside me that insists I should be out doing weekendy things. Like visiting the growers' market! And playing in the park! And having a picnic! Or going to the museum! Maybe a gallery! And the zoo! How about the aquarium! Why don't I throw a dinner party! Book a farm stay! Or do papier-mâché! Have my in-laws over for brunch! Invite some girlfriends for afternoon tea with lamingtons! Homemade! Boo-yah!

Of course I do none of this because I can't be bothered

and I'm not organised enough. And then the guilt peaks and I start feeling inadequate. I begin worrying our weekends aren't fun or interesting enough and that's somehow damaging to my family. Why, I'm not entirely sure but there's little point letting logic get in the way of a good guilt trip.

Here's another First World Problem for you: when you spend your weekdays juggling work and family it can be jarring to shift to a single focus on weekends. I try to put strict boundaries and barbed wire fences around my weekends in a desperate bid to quarantine 'home time' from 'work time'. In theory, I don't check my emails, I don't surf, I try not to look at Mamamia, and I stay off Twitter.

In practice, I suck. In weak moments I will invariably clamber over the razor wire separating home from work and stagger, slashed, bleeding and desperate, towards the Internet. I blame my iPhone for this because I'm not carrying around a phone any more – I'm carrying around a damn computer. I love it but it tempts me so.

There are other challenges that come with being at home full time on the weekend. With work, no matter how overwhelmed I am, how utterly swamped with demands and deadlines and disasters urgently needing to be averted, there is still a level of order, no matter how tenuous.

Allow me to be specific. In my work life, nobody vomits into my hair. Nobody flatly refuses to get dressed because 'clothes touching my body makes me ITCH-YYYYYY!!' Nobody puts my shoes in the toilet. Compared to all that, the demands of my working week follow a satisfying degree of logic and order. Because there is no order with small children. Nor logic. Not in my house anyway. Not when I'm in charge.

After kids, your weekends change entirely. I'm not complaining about this or wishing it was different but let's be honest: all the things you traditionally associated with weekends – sleeping in, late nights, reading newspapers over brunch – are gone. Poof. Bye-bye. In their place is forty-eight hours of intense.

For parents who work outside the house, the weekend can be a welcome opportunity to do the quality time thing. For stay-at-home parents it can bring an influx of extra support in the form of a partner. Alternatively – for single parents, say – it can be hard work. Ditto all the golf, cricket, cycling and sailing widows whose partners spend weekends doing hours of sport, leaving them holding the fort and often the kids.

***

When I was a kid, one of our weekend family traditions was going to the supermarket. It's hard to believe now but, back then, shops were only open on Saturday mornings until 12, so for people who worked and couldn't duck out on a Thursday night, this was your only option.

My mum was never a supermarket shopper. She always hated it, and whether by choice or necessity, my dad picked up that mantle. We went together, to Franklins because it was the cheapest, with our list and our rituals. I would put Coco Pops in the trolley. He would take them out and replace them with Sultana Bran. I would put white bread in the trolley and he would replace it with Vogel's – Mum's orders.

It was a companionable time and we both enjoyed spending it together. Sadly, I have not maintained this tradition with my own children because the supermarket has become a battleground for me. Take me there without blinkers, a detailed list and a strict time limit, and I will wander the aisles for hours, dazed and confused.

There are just Too Many Things. Like baked beans. As if brand and can size weren't troublesome enough, I'm now forced into more decisions. Salt-reduced? Ham? Weight Watchers? BBQ? Organic? Sausages? Steak & Bacon? Rich Tomato? Cheese Sauce? English Recipe?

I don't have *time* for this. They're *baked beans*. And I'm trying to have *a life*. There should just be one type: Heinz. Normal. Medium-sized can. The end.

Bread is worse. It used to just be bread. White. Tip Top. Vogel's if you were a bit hippy like my mum. Now the bread aisle stretches 100 metres and you must consider things you never knew could go in bread, like oat bran, pumpkin seeds, iron, soy, linseed and omega-3. Isn't that fish oil? Do I really want fish with my bread? Well, yes, maybe I do. Do I?

Because all these fancy-pants ingredients make you feel negligent if you choose the bread *without* the fish.

It's enough to give you a panic attack. My favourite place in a supermarket to feel anxious is in front of the feminine hygiene products. Buying them always makes me slightly squirmy. I know we're all adults and I should get over it but I can't. The squirm factor has been amped up recently because there are now a gazillion different types. *'Dear Tampon and Pad Companies, I do not feel empowered and liberated by having so many choices. I feel mildly embarrassed, overwhelmed and cranky. Okay?'*

In simpler times, you could quickly identify what you needed, sweep it into your trolley with barely a reduction in speed, nudge it discreetly under the bread-without-fish and keep on trucking down the aisle towards dishwashing detergent.

But now? Now you must stand there conspicuously for twenty minutes weighing up the relative benefits of bizarre words like 'wings', 'aloe', 'breathable', 'flexia', 'silk', 'barely there', 'body fit' and 'invisible' while your fellow shoppers trudge past with knowing smirks. You may as well be wearing a T-shirt saying, 'Hello! I Menstruate And I'm Confused!'

Milk also has become a problem. When did it become so complicated? One troubling day I counted six different types of it in my fridge. This is preposterous because there are only five different types of people in my house. Somehow, we had Shape for me, Lite White for my son, Lite Soy for my husband, Full Cream for my daughter and expressed breast milk for the baby.

On this particular day, there was also rice milk. I'm unsure how it got there and it remains unclaimed. Looking for something to put in your tea? Approach my fridge with extreme caution. One slip of the hand and you may know more about lactation than any adult should . . .

When I was little, milk came in bottles. Hi-Lo was the only – impossibly exotic – variation. Life was simpler then. Less choice, more headspace. Now, the explosion of options in every category of grocery item is doing my head in and not just because I am an indecisive Libran.

Homewares shops are equally challenging. They overwhelm me like supermarkets. Several years ago when I was selling my house, we did that thing where you tart it up for the inspections. In a bid to infuse it with some style I did not have, I asked a friend to come over and give it a joosh. 'You need some monkey balls in a bowl on this coffee table,' she pronounced. I nodded as if I'd known that all along. She told me where to find them and the next day I made my Monkey Ball Pilgrimage. It was to one of those fancy homewares shops, the type that makes men want to dash to the nearest hardware store and buy a chainsaw to replenish their testosterone levels. There's a word in Yiddish that describes its contents perfectly: *chochkes*, which roughly translates as small, decorative objects that collect dust.

After twenty horrible minutes, this is the message I hissed into my friend's voicemail: 'I'm here looking for monkey balls and, well, *what the hell is a monkey ball*? I thought I'd recognise one when I saw it but now I'm just having a panic attack. Maybe "monkey balls" is just a euphemism for any kind of small object you can fill a bowl with? In that case I'm stuffed because there are dozens of bowl-stuffers here.

Are they these kind of silver things or are those Christmas decorations? What about shells? Can they be monkey balls or do they have to be round? Ceramic? Paper? Shit, gotta go, no oxygen, *call me!*'

The call came too late. I was never going back to that shop. Instead, I filled the bowl with lemons. Lemons are good. They only come in one type.

Once upon a time, I may have used those lemons to make a cake after they'd done their job in the bowl. I binge on cooking. Not on the food so much but on the actual act of cooking. I'll go through a frenzy of buying ingredients and baking and collecting recipes and then I'll drop it. For years.

One night, during one of my cooking blackouts, I was making dinner. Yes, I know. Riveting. Actually, it was a pretty exciting situation for my family because they rarely get decent home-cooked meals. I haven't had a cooking binge in . . . oh, about two children.

So there I was, feeling pretty smug about the fact I'd defrosted a lamb rack and was going to roast it with some potatoes. Frozen peas were my final key ingredient.

But when I took the rack out of the packaging and went to put it in the baking tray, it was just . . . so . . . tiny. It broke my heart, thinking about the size of those little ribs. And then I began to cry. Who cries while they're trying to make dinner? Seriously, *who does that?*

'I can't do this,' I announced dramatically before fleeing the kitchen. Someone else finished cooking the lamb that night and I ate scrambled eggs.

My career in vegetarianism has been very patchy and characterised by inconsistency and gross hypocrisy. It began as soon as I learned what veal was, around age twelve. The thought of eating a little milk-fed calf turned my stomach and killed my appetite. Bye-bye schnitzel. This was followed swiftly by lamb and things progressed from there until, by seventeen, I wasn't eating any red meat at all. I maintained this position for a decade and for many of those years I didn't eat chicken either.

Then one day, after ten years of no red meat, I had a mouthful of lasagne at a friend's house and the dam burst. Over the next few months, I scurried back up the food chain until I was once again eating most meat except veal. I've never eaten things like duck or rabbit or deer because I relate to those animals in a way I don't relate to chickens – perhaps because many of them were storybook characters. Bambi, anyone?

My approach to meat eating has always been heavy on denial – I need my food not to look like an animal. I don't like blood. I don't like shapes that resemble body parts. That's probably why I can wear leather. Shoes do not look like cows. Neither do jackets.

Lately, little things are pushing me back down the vegetarian path. Like the lamb rack. And the YouTube video someone sent me featuring a tiny pet piglet whose owner took it to the beach on a leash. It was so adorable my computer nearly ovulated. At the markets recently, I wandered past one of those baby animal farms. I stood for ages watching the little piglets and calves, transfixed by their cuteness. We had vegetarian pad Thai for dinner that night.

If I had more discipline and conviction, I would stop eating meat altogether. It's a decision I struggle with at most meals. Sometimes the animals win. Sometimes my taste-buds do.

Wherever you sit on the meat-eating spectrum, please do not be defensive. By telling you how I feel about eating meat, I am not implicitly criticising your position. This is not about telling *you* what to eat. Or wear. Or think.

All the vegetarians I know are very low key about their choice not to eat meat. None of them rams tofu down your throat in a bid to convert you. But I've noticed many meat-eaters will take someone else's decision not to eat meat as a thrown-down gauntlet.

Hunting for chinks in the vegetarian's ethical armour, the meat-eater's first question is always, 'Do you wear leather shoes?' They tend to issue this challenge snidely, confident it's the killer punch that will deliver an instant moral victory. Many vegetarians or semi-vegetarians or wannabe vegetarians do wear leather shoes. My hand is up. I have several leather jackets and belts. I even have a pair of leather pants that I impulsively bought one day when I was feeling a bit rock 'n' roll. But fur of any kind? Even possum? Rabbit? Forgeddaboudit.

Everyone has different lines about what they eat and wear. These lines may shift over a lifetime or even a day. For some it's 'anything with a face'. For others it's 'anything with a mother'. Some won't touch red meat but are cool with everything else. Others eat only seafood. Some people will wear leather but not fur. Some will only wear certain kinds of fur. Others eat everything except rabbits because the idea of chowing down on a bunny is too confronting.

Then there are those vegetarians who turn a blind eye to a doner kebab when blind themselves at 3 a.m. Whatever.

Someone's choice about what they're comfortable eating is a personal one, not to be mocked or disparaged just because your choice is different.

I did have a chuckle the other day when I heard someone say, 'If God didn't intend us to eat animals, he wouldn't have made them from meat.' Clearly, that's my problem.

Christmas is certainly a problem if you're a turkey. Bad, bad time to be a turkey, December. And turkeys aren't the only ones who dread it.

'Tis the season to have a nervous breakdown. Seriously. There is no more stressful time of year and what makes it worse, I think, is how we're all meant to be so ho bloody ho and filled with cheer. So without going all bah-humbug on you (I do love Christmas, mostly), I thought I'd take a moment to acknowledge some un-jolly aspects of the silly season . . .

1. EXPECTING TOO MUCH. Here's the thing: Christmas peaks around age four to six. The excitement, the magic, the presents. The lack of responsibility. All you have to do is show up and open gifts. The rest of your life will be spent eating, drinking and incurring vast credit card debt to try to recapture that elusive magic. You never will. I'm just saying.

2. PLAYING HAPPY FAMILIES. Blended families can be a wonderful thing. So can in-laws. No so much on December 25th. The collision of geography, logistics and family politics is ugly. In many households, complex negotiations begin months out. 'We went to your parents last year,' it goes. 'This year we have to have lunch with my mum and then drop in to see my dad, even though I can't stand my step-mother's kids and their annoying brats who never say thankyou for their presents.' So much time in the car. So much turkey and beer in the stomach. So much reverting to dysfunctional childhood roles.

The only thing worse is having lost someone you love and feeling their loss even more acutely at Christmas. Are we having fun yet?

3. KEEPING SANTA ALIVE. Once your children reach a certain age, you have to work the Santa thing so much harder. Annoyingly, kids today are smarter than we were and they start questioning the viability of the big guy in the red suit earlier than we ever did. However, there is a crucial kiddie grey zone between unflinching belief and knowing for sure Santa is bollocks.

My parents, bless them, stuffed this up. I'M NOT AT ALL EMOTIONALLY SCARRED by this, but I clearly remember the day Santa died. I was about nine, and for the first time on Christmas morning there was no present from Santa under our tree. When I questioned this, my parents cheerfully said, 'Come on, darling, no more Santa presents.' There were many other presents but I burst into tears and was quite inconsolable. Sure, I knew the idea of a dude in a suit shimmying down our chimney was fairly outlandish but I wasn't ready to have this confirmed. NOT DAMAGED THOUGH. NOT ME.

I have one friend whose Santa-Is-Real-Oh-Yes-He-Is! pantomime grows more elaborate every year as her children become more suspicious and she more desperate to keep the magic alive. Here's how she tells it: 'Kids over eight know if the stationery from the North Pole is actually from Mummy's desk drawer. This means separate pen, separate paper and disguised handwriting. Xmas Eve we leave milk and cookies for Santa and carrots for the reindeer. Once the kids are asleep, we wrap presents with Xmas paper they haven't seen (see above). Next we nibble on the carrots and leave a trail of cookie and carrot crumbs from under the tree to the chimney. Outside, we leave reindeer prints – light a match, let it burn all the way down and then use the charcoal to replicate little reindeer prints outside on the path.'

Needless to say, all this is far more challenging when drunk, so Christmas Eve parties are best avoided when your kids are small.

4. HAVING A DRINK WITH EVERYONE YOU'VE EVER MET. It starts in November: all those noises about 'getting together before Christmas'. Why? I haven't seen you for months. Years sometimes. Why do I have to see you now? I used to panic about this, feel pressured by all the invitations and threats of invitations. Then I realised you just go along with it and make agreeable noises and nothing happens. Just like the rest of the year. The key is to be positive yet non-specific. Say 'Oh yes, totally, we must have a drink' while thinking 'How about never? Is never good for you?'

5. SPENDING UNTIL IT HURTS AND THEN SPENDING SOME MORE. The best Christmas shopping experience I ever had was wandering around Target at 11 p.m. one night a few days before Christmas. At all other times, there's a feeling of white-knuckle panic as you dash around maniacally grabbing things you don't need and nobody wants. This feeling intensifies the closer you get to 6 p.m. on Christmas Eve, which looms large as some kind of ominous deadline. My thinking goes like this: 'After 6 p.m., I'll never again in my life be able to buy anything so I'd better

purchase every item in the world in case I need some of it.' This is despite the fact that convenience stores and other shops are now open on Christmas Day. Then not only do all shops re-open on Boxing Day, but everything in the world is on sale.

There is a void in my brain where this logic lives, so every year I find myself stocking up like one of those contestants on a game show where you have sixty seconds to fill your shopping trolley for free. Except it's not free.

Recently, all this spending has been overlaid with a strong sense of guilt that we're contributing to the destruction of the planet by buying and wrapping a bunch of unnecessary shit. Does the world really need more scented candles?

Ho ho help.

Life With Children

'I'm having a caesarean to keep my girly parts pristine,' announced the heavily pregnant woman I'd just met. 'I booked in as soon as I found out my due date.'

There we were at a fashion show back in my magazine days and I was chatting with a few friends and acquaintances. When caesar-woman joined the group, small talk naturally swung to pregnancy. Then she dropped her clanger.

As we clutched our drinks that little bit tighter in the stunned silence, she merrily picked up her shovel and kept digging. *You know*,' she emphasised conspiratorially, 'so I don't get all stretched and floppy *down there*.'

Oh my lord, it's happened, I marvelled, while wrestling my urge to smack her. I've finally met a real-life woman who's

Too Posh To Push. I thought they were an urban myth. Or a Hollywood truth. But regular women? Who knew!

Fortunately, at that moment we were ushered to our seats and the conversation ended. But as the models flounced down the catwalk in their pretty summer frocks, I started obsessing. 'Why am I so cross with that stupid woman?' I asked my friend afterwards. 'Because she insulted us,' she replied. 'By telling everyone she's having a caesar to preserve her vagina, she's basically saying all women who've given birth vaginally are stretched, floppy and like the Grand Canyon.'

Yes, that's exactly why I was pissed. Step down, bitch. I won't be having you diss my lady garden, nuh-uh.

'What makes it even worse is that it's an impossible thing to defend,' continued my friend. 'If you try to explain how it all snaps back and that your partner is perfectly happy, you can tell she's thinking, "Yeah sure. He only tells you that because he wants to have sex with you. He's lying and you're the Grand Canyon and I pity you." More champagne?'

Over the next few days, still grumpy, I re-told the story to other mothers who were similarly pissed.

'Before giving birth to my first child, my bloody dentist told me, "sex will never be the same" and suggested a caesar,' huffed one friend. 'I asked in what way specifically would it be different and he said, "Well, mainly it impacts on your husband . . . most men I speak to agree." I wonder if this is a medically proven fact or a conversation he'd had on the golf course, being the insightful sixty-something *dentist* he was. I managed to have sex often enough to get pregnant three times in two years, so I guess my husband had no complaints!'

And this from a friend who gave birth last year: 'After twenty hours of labour followed by an emergency caesar, I tell you they could have pulled my child out of my nose at that point and I wouldn't have objected – the state of my girl parts was the last thing on my mind. We didn't have sex again for about four months by which time my husband would have jumped at the opportunity even if there had been a grenade up there. If he was disappointed, he forgot to mention it through his enormous post-coital grin.'

But enough from the ladies. I decided to ask a couple of single blokes who've dated women with kids for their honest appraisal of the vaginal situation. I figured this would circumvent any accusation of bias based on the self-interest of men asked the same question by the mothers of their children. You know, men who would like to have sex again with their wives and also retain two testicles.

I'm pleased to report that both my single male survey subjects do not think that good sex and vaginal birth are mutually exclusive events. 'Hell no, you can't tell the difference,' insisted one. 'Every woman is different anyway, kids or not.'

Interesting. So, vaginas are like snowflakes? Or something.

'Any guy who complains is just making excuses for his own shortcomings,' confirmed the other guy, amusing himself for a good five minutes with his wit. No Grand Canyon? 'No Grand Canyon.'

I've not had a sun-roof birth but several women I know who've given birth both ways say it's bollocks to assume a caesar is the easy option. 'I was standing up in the shower half an hour after having my first son vaginally,' said one mother. 'But I had to have a caesar with my second and I could barely move for two days. The pain was awful and the recovery was longer than I'd expected. It's not like getting a Brazilian. It's major surgery.'

Another friend who had to have an emergency caesarean after two natural births is more blunt: 'Sure, babies are meant to come out of vaginas. But thank God we're blessed in this modern age to have medical options. Without them, my last baby would have died. And I might have too. Making birth about vaginal vanity is insane.'

They don't discuss caesareans or vaginal vanity in *Where Did I Come From?* Maybe they should. Perhaps you recall that book. It was instrumental in my early sex education and perhaps also in yours. Now that many of us have children ourselves, it's been reprinted, as parents have decided to use it to explain sex to a new generation of curious kids. Ah, nostalgia. Remember those cute illustrations of the sperm?

Small problem: *Where Did I Come From?* needs an urgent software upgrade, as does the whole birds-and-bees concept.

A girlfriend discovered this the hard way during a conversation with her nine-year-old daughter not long ago. 'We'd just finished reading *Where Did I Come From?*, which I'd bought on Amazon, and I was congratulating myself on getting through it without either of us giggling inappropriately,' she told me. 'Then I asked Chloe if she had any questions and straight away she hits me with this: "Mum, how do lesbians have babies?"'

To her credit, my friend didn't miss a beat and carefully explained the various ways two women might make a baby. I think she should have been grateful that the last word of her daughter's question was 'babies' and not 'sex'. Because for an uncomfortable moment, it could have gone either way. 'I wasn't quite ready to explain oral sex and strap-ons,' she admits honestly.

Look, she shouldn't have been that surprised to find herself discussing turkey basters, sperm banks and IVF with a nine-year-old. We have mutual lesbian friends with a baby so gay procreation is in our kids' orbit. Which is a good thing, I believe. Like most kids these days, my friend's daughter already knows stuff we only discovered when we were decades older.

The Sex Talk has certainly changed since we had it with our own parents. 'My mother sat me down with this pastel watercolour book with weird pictures,' remembers a Catholic friend, the eldest of five. 'It was all very formal and I thought quite revolting. Very uptight and serious. A very Catholic mother doing her best to discuss a subject she had never had a conversation about in her entire life with anyone. All too embarrassing because actually no one ever has sex in Catholic families! They just have children!'

'I learnt about sex in a panic,' remembers another friend. 'A precocious girl at school set me up with a date and warned me I would have to kiss him. I thought that was fine at the time because I regularly kissed my dog, so how bad could a boy be? Then, at the party, just before "the time", my friend dropped the bombshell that my mouth would need to be open. OPEN??? I mean how did *that* work? She then mentioned tongue and I think I had a pubescent panic attack and left.'

'I never got a sex talk. I learnt about it through the thin walls of my parents' room,' recalls another friend. 'As I got a little older, I had to sleep with a pillow over my head. My mother was a yeller so for a long time I worried that sex sounded awfully painful. She never ever spoke to me about it despite being very liberal and progressive in other ways. So I had to fill in the blanks about sex without much success. I believed if you ate a pip from an apple or a watermelon it would grow into a baby inside you. And I practised kissing with my friend and thought I was going to get an STD, although I wasn't quite sure what that meant. But it sounded nasty and I was worried.'

'My sex education came from going to the riding camp,' a 38-year-old guy friend told me. 'There were boys and girls from seven right up to twenty. I learnt a lot from all the kids there, like the fact that girls got periods and used things called tampons to block themselves up. As little boys we thought this was pretty freaky. Later, we played catch and pash and eventually I felt my first boob.'

Another male friend simply absorbed '70s popular culture. 'I learnt a lot through listening to music like the Radiators, who sung 'Gimme Head', or Frank Zappa singing about Catholic girls and what they got up to. Even *The Rocky Horror Picture Show* enlightened me. So by the time I was ready to hit the park and start exploring girls' nether regions I was a little prepared. Actually, I don't think I've progressed very far since . . .'

My memory of my own Sex Talk is crystal clear. I was about nine and keen to know how babies were made. My mother, a feminist, decided it was important for me to know how my body worked so she talked me through the whole shebang from sex to pregnancy, labour and birth.

One memorable point was that, in those days, women were routinely given enemas when they went into labour in order to . . . clear things out before they had to push.

I remember listening attentively and when she was finished I sat quietly for a moment, taking it all in. And then: 'I think that all sounds okay, except for the part with the man's penis and the enema. They sound yucky.'

So what's changed since *we* learnt about sex? Two things.

Via the Internet, music videos, rap lyrics, train-wreck celebrities, reality TV and news and current affairs shows, kids
are exposed to a million things we weren't. This is generally
not terrific.

But happily, social mores have evolved a long way since
we were kids, so that once taboo topics like homosexuality,
miscarriage and infertility have gained widespread acceptance. The result? The facts of life aren't what they used to
be. Oh no. After the baby-making basics, there are some
very modern addendums.

One friend's eight-year-old son wanted to know about
IVF. He'd heard the term in conversation and on TV and was
wondering if it stood for 'International Vagina Foundation'.
No, but perhaps it should.

And don't forget safe sex. Generation X parents, thoroughly scarred by the Grim Reaper campaign of our youth,
have to throw in a mandatory P.S. about condoms.

Having made a simple yet impassioned speech to her
ten-year-old about the importance of safe sex, one friend's
son asked, 'Okay, but where do people buy condoms from?'
When she replied that they were sold in chemists and supermarkets, he was incredulous. 'No WAY! But I've been to
Woollies loads of times and I've never seen them!'

Such a rude thing in such a normal place! Who knew? I remember being similarly amazed to discover the words 'sex' and 'penis' were in the dictionary. Such rude words in such a dull book.

Then there are the mandatory warnings about sex and technology, something most parents haven't a clue about and really should. 'My twelve-year-old knows about sex because we've had talks about it over the last few years, but the other day I found myself saying to him sternly, "Never send a girl a photo of your penis over the phone or Internet, okay?"' one friend who does understand technology told me. 'I also had to tell him that if a girl ever sent him a nude or topless photo that he had to delete it immediately or he could be charged with possession of child pornography. That certainly got his attention.'

This is true. Since kids are not the greatest comprehenders of consequences until it's too late, it's crucial to talk them through what could happen if they drink too much and let someone they trust take a photo of them in a compromising position. With a couple of clicks it could be all around their school and even all around the world. And you can't get it back.

Are we having fun yet, parents?

Right. So, let's re-cap. Lesbians? Turkey basters? Con-doms? Strap-ons? Sexting? IVF?

As liberated and laid-back as you think you are, you're suddenly not when it's your own child and the words 'penis', 'vagina' and 'very special grown-up cuddle' have to come out of your mouth.

I acquitted myself very badly when my daughter asked me about sex when I was pregnant with her little brother. Because I'd written dozens of sealed sections detailing every possible permutation of the sexual act, I always assumed I'd be more prepared than most when it came to 'the talk'. Wrong.

I discovered this the hard way when my three-year-old asked, 'But how did the baby get inside your tummy, Mummy?'

Not content to let it rest with the sperm and egg basics, my little girl wanted transport details: how *exactly* did Daddy's sperm get inside Mummy?

In my mind, I'd always imagined how this conversation would go. My image was of me being the cool, modern mum, telling my daughter about sex in plain language and mak-ing sure I portrayed it as a positive, natural thing between two loving people. Just like my mum had done when she'd explained it to me.

But when the moment came, I got nervous and flustered and started giggling, much to my horror. When I finally pulled myself together, I blurted something lame about special cuddles and asked if she wanted some ice cream with sprinkles in a desperate attempt at sugar diversion. Then off I went to look for my dog-eared copy of *Where Did I Come From?*

And if you were worried about not giving enough information, you should also worry about giving too much. Terrific. Child experts recommend you feed kids very small pieces of info as they request it, instead of launching into a full-blown explanation from a standing start.

This happened to a friend whose eleven-year-old son announced one morning over breakfast that, during the night, he thought he'd had a spurt and it hurt a bit. 'My wife and I began stumbling over each other in our awkward attempts to explain it was nothing to be concerned about and that it could happen while you were asleep and that this sort of thing was common for young boys and blah blah blah,' my friend told me. 'As we babbled, he looked increasingly puzzled and when we finally realised we were possibly delving too deeply into the subject and shut up, we asked if he had any questions. He looked thoughtful before saying, "Well, how long will I be having these growth spurts? Because I want to get taller but my legs are really quite sore."'

Fear not! If older kids don't learn about sex from books or parents, the playground will disseminate the information for them. The bad news is that this can be rather hit and miss. I don't remember talking much about it at school when I was six but today's little kids have turned sex into a verb: sexing. If pressed, they're not entirely sure what sexing means but they know it's kind of rude and thus good to throw around in playground conversation for a bit of cred or shock value.

Remember playing kiss and catch? It's still popular among the littlies, although with one notable difference: there are strict rules at most co-ed schools about kissing. It's not allowed. Completely banned. And this isn't to protect the girls; it's more likely to be small boys who need shelter from their eager pursuers.

Rules aside, nothing's changed in that respect. In those early primary years, girls have always been the instigators. I remember having my first crush on a boy at school when I was five. His name was Joel and I used to make him play Superman, where he was Superman and I was a distressed damsel whom he had to rescue from the silver metal seats where I pretended to be tied up. Invariably, he'd quickly grow bored and wander off to play tips with the other boys. It took me quite some time to accept that Joel Just Wasn't That Into Me.

A generation later, when my son was about five, I watched him grow exasperated when his friend Mimi kept insisting they play 'marriages'. 'How do you play that?' I inquired. He grimaced as if in physical pain. 'Oh it's awful. You just have to do lots of slow dancing and hugging and stuff. I hate it.'

SNAGs 0, blokes 1.

Here's something else they don't tell you in the parenting books: the most important conversations you'll have with your kids will be in the car. While driving. That's when they'll choose to mess with your head, throw you their curliest questions and make their most jaw-dropping observations. This will be both good and bad.

Good because from the backseat, they can't see the panic in your eyes. Bad because when you're freaking out, it can be hard not to crash into a tree.

I'm not talking factual questions like, 'Why do some trees lose their leaves in autumn and others don't?' That's what Google and smart phones are for. Just pass your phone back to your kid who will be able to find the answer before the lights go green. Even if he's four. The *true* challenges are your more esoteric dilemmas. Birth, death, religion, politics, sex. All the topics that make a dinner party lively, but not ideal to discuss with a six-year-old while trying to remember whether you're passing through a 40 kilometres per hour school zone.

When you're confronted with explaining Big Issues, the responsibility of being a parent weighs heavily because you're meant to have the answers and often you don't. Not when put on the spot, anyway. These are the times when you can almost hear the drum roll as the universe waits for you to bugger it up and wreck your kid's life. That's how important it feels. The consequence of the wrong response is, naturally, a lifetime of therapy for your child. NO PRESSURE. Add a moving vehicle to the equation and it makes for some merry hell.

Whenever I'm faced with one of those drumroll moments, there are two images that flash into my head. One is of Russell Crowe in *Romper Stomper*, an angry skinhead roaming the streets causing mindless havoc, no doubt as a result of something his parents once said to him. The other is of my child as an adult, lying on a couch while talking to a therapist about how the root of all their life's problems was me. Both images fill me with dread. Given that my view of therapy is not a bad one, I should clarify that it's not the therapy that disturbs me but rather the idea that the root of all my child's future problems will be traced back to this one conversation where I stuffed it. NO PRESSURE.

Every parent has a Car Conversation that is seared into their memory. Like the friend who was driving her seven-year-old home from school while they casually chatted about his day. It was the usual stuff. Why he wished he could have had a jam sandwich instead of cheese and lettuce. How much he'd enjoyed PE. And then this: 'You know, Mum, at lunchtime, Ruby came up to me in the playground and said she'd heard a rumour I was gay.' Pause. 'So . . . I called her a lesbian.'

Hello, tree? I'm coming for you.

My friend explained. 'I was torn between bursting out laughing and delivering a stern lecture on the evils of homosexual vilification.' She went with a diligent attempt at the lecture, which went really well if her intention had been to dig herself into a really big hole. 'Sweetie, you know, there's nothing wrong with being gay.'

'But, Mum, I'm not gay.'

'Well, okay, but we absolutely must not call someone gay or lesbian in a mean way.'

'But, Mum, you said there was nothing wrong with being a lesbian so why does it matter that I called her one?'

'Oh. Yes. I did, didn't I? Because there *is* nothing wrong with being a lesbian or gay but well . . .'

Try explaining your way out of that one while operating heavy machinery. I dare you.

When my own son was about five, he piped up with this pearler from his booster seat, apropos nothing: 'Mum, what does God wear?'

Anyone?

Ingeniously, I reached for the emergency parenting technique called Answering A Question With Another Question To Buy Yourself Some Time. 'Um, well, sweetheart, when you think about God, what is he wearing in your mind?' Nice save. I considered myself lucky he didn't throw in a follow-up question about Richard Dawkins' theories on atheism.

One day, while driving home from a Fairies concert, it was my daughter's turn. Basking in the happy glow of some mother–daughter time, I was blind-sided when my three-year-old piped up from the back seat, 'Mummy, I think the green fairy looked a bit fat.'

Gulp. As I tried to focus on the road, my voice

inadvertently raised a few octaves as I gaily replied, 'Oh no she didn't, darling!'

'Yes, she did. In her tummy. Maybe she was pregnant.'

Dear Lord, are we there already? Am I really having a conversation with my daughter about body image? At three? While simultaneously trying to follow my sat-nav? By the way, the fairy she was referring to was about a size 12. Not fat. Not pregnant.

'No, darling, I don't think she was fat at all! I think she looked LOVELY!' And then? I found myself uttering the following words, my voice borderline hysterical with desperate enthusiasm and fervent passion: 'You know, fairies come in all shapes and sizes!'

At that point, she shut down and didn't want to talk any more and I was ready for some therapy of my own.

A few weeks later, I went shopping with a girlfriend. We didn't mean to shop. We meant to drink coffee and eat cake. I can prove this because we had some of our children with us and everyone knows children are shopping's mortal enemy. No sane person would ever willingly choose to try on clothes while accompanied by anyone too young to drive. It's insanity meets extreme sport with a dollop of masochism on top to seal the deal.

Giddy with caffeine and sugar, however, we decided we could totally handle popping into one little boutique on the way back to the car. While my friend ducked into the fitting room to try on a dress, I flicked distractedly through the racks while trying to watch three children with two eyes. You do the maths.

After approximately one hundred years, my friend emerged from behind the curtain with a look on her face that was part rage, part mortification. I recognised that look. It meant there was no mirror inside the change-room and she wanted to hurt the boutique owner very badly before cowering under the nearest chair.

As she stood self-consciously in front of the poxy public mirror, checking out her reflection, she called for some input on the dress. 'Is it too short?' she asked me.

'No,' I assured her. 'Not at all.' She wasn't convinced. 'Your legs look great!' Still not. 'Look, it's not like I can see your vagina or anything.'

As we were talking, the kids had gathered to loudly inform us they wanted to leave. Having caught the end of our conversation, my friend's four-year-old daughter began to chant, 'Va-GINA, Va-GINA, Va-GINA, Va-GINA,' while leaping about doing ballet on the shop floor.

Naturally, being a mature adult, I burst out laughing. But my friend was cross. With me. 'Thanks a LOT!' she muttered under her breath while looking like she wanted to smack me about the head with a wooden coathanger. I was baffled.

'What?' I asked, trying to stop giggling.

'We don't use that word,' she hissed back at me.

'You mean vagina?' She nodded. 'Well, what do you call it?' I replied.

'We call it a "La-La",' she said.

I blinked. 'What, like the Teletubby?'

She wasn't amused and we abandoned our shopping shortly afterwards, with the sound of the 'Va-GINA' chant ringing in our ears as we headed home. See what can happen when you mix caffeine, sugar, shopping and kids?

In my family, we were taught to call genitals by their proper names. Just like any other noun or body part. My mother believed it was important that we knew what was what. In public, we did occasionally use the euphemisms 'front bottom' and 'back bottom', but from very early on I knew the proper names for all the bits. Yes, I know that technically the 'vagina' is what the inside is called and the outside is called the 'vulva' but I still think vagina is better than La-La, okay?

I've since discovered this is a philosophy not everybody shares. There are many people who aren't comfortable with the correct anatomical words for male and female genitals. Then there are all those people who, after they become parents, just fall into cutesy nicknames in the same way baby-talk causes you to dumb down all kinds of words until you find yourself in an adult conversation referring to din-dins and reminding yourself you need to buy milkies on the way home.

So why the reluctance to call genitals by their proper names? And by encouraging kids to use terms like La-La or Shiny or Wee-Wee, what are we actually teaching them about their bodies?

Granted, the real words are not terribly pretty but we're yet to settle on widely accepted substitutes, at least not when it comes to women.

As writer Suzy Freeman-Greene once wrote in an article about the increasing number of women electing to have cosmetic surgery on their genitals, '. . . as the shape of the vagina becomes a crazy new source of angst, we still don't even have an affectionate word to describe it. Where is the cosy, non-threatening equivalent to "willy"? This linguistic absence speaks volumes about social attitudes towards female genitalia. Meanwhile, the c-word endures as a form of abuse.'

This is true, although I'd like to take a moment to cast my vote for 'lady garden' and 'va-jay-jay' – two of my favourite euphemisms.

Perhaps the most compelling and sobering reason for teaching kids the proper words comes from child-protection experts. They site research showing that many kids don't report 'rude' behaviour because they're worried about using 'rude' words that could get them into trouble. They also point out that if a child goes to a teacher or another adult to tell them something inappropriate has occurred, it's important they be easily understood. Saying 'Joey touched my Shiny' might not get the point across clearly enough.

One thing most people can agree on is boobs. Or what to call them anyway. I find the word 'boobs' pretty much gets your point across to anyone of any age and at any time.

For things that are so common, I'm still always surprised when a little flare of controversy springs up around boobs, something that tends to happen every so often with boring predictability.

Unless you're a stripper, there are only two times in life when you're likely to get your boobs out in public: breast-feeding and topless sunbathing. Over the years, I've done my fair share of both, although, admittedly, the more I've done of the former, the less I've done of the latter. Dear Gravity, you are a goddamn cow.

I once read that 37 per cent of people believe breast-feeding should only occur at home or in toilet cubicles. I wonder if those same people would say the same about topless sunbathing?

I also wonder how they feel about celebrities and super-models baring their breasts at parties and photo shoots. Unacceptable? Oh yes. And hurry, Miranda, your inappropriate breasts are offending my eyes.

If my eldest son had been surveyed, he would have immediately ticked the box that said 'Breastfeeding should only happen at home and preferably inside a dark cupboard'. He's always cringed when I've fed his younger siblings in public, despite having had no complaints when he was a hungry baby himself. How quickly they forget.

You may still recall the hype when media personality Kate Langbroek breastfed on live TV during *The Panel*. 'Publicity stunt!' cried some. 'Outrageous!' cried others. 'Oh please!' I cried at nobody in particular. There's nothing contrived about breastfeeding. If only infants could follow a PR schedule. Have you met a baby? They tend to be rather spontaneous and extremely unreasonable, particularly when tired or hungry, which is approximately always. Kate Langbroek was at work. Her baby was hungry. She fed him. It happens. The end. And yet people still talk about it nearly a decade later.

The fact that she was working at all is a problem for some people, who feel uncomfortable when the worlds of work and motherhood collide. They can't compute that personal choice or financial necessity makes that collision a reality for millions of women every day. Oh look, it's not the 1950s any more!

With over a decade of breastfeeding on my CV (not continuously and not of the same child . . . no Bitty in our house), there's not a public place where I haven't breastfed or expressed. Beaches, planes, shopping centres, parks, boats, lifts, airports, restaurants, barbecues, offices, cafés, meetings, parties, weddings, funerals, churches, synagogues . . . and frankly, I couldn't have cared less who was watching.

Oddly enough, I always tended to prioritise my baby's immediate needs over the Elizabethan prudishness of people who have a problem with boobs being used for their natural function. I'm whacky like that.

When I'm in breastfeeding mode, my breasts are about as sexual to me as a bowl of All Bran. Because that's exactly what they represent to my baby. Sustenance. Not sex.

I also find the term 'public breastfeeding' amusing. Those who oppose it exude a fearful, vaguely alarmed vibe, as if there are groups of marauding mothers using their babies as an excuse to flash their lactating breasts in strangers' faces: 'I know! Let's meet at Westfield! The first person to flash their leaky nipple to a hundred shoppers wins a toasted focaccia!'

As for the suggestion by some that breastfeeding should happen in toilets, I totally agree. As soon as those same people are happy to have their morning coffee made, served and drunk in a toilet cubicle, we shall happily breastfeed right alongside them.

My other favourite thing is when people say mothers should be discreet. I have to agree with this too. There are far too many breastfeeding women who brazenly strip naked to the waist in public each time their baby grizzles. Have you seen them throw their bosoms around with gay abandon while waving their arms in the air like they just don't care? What is wrong with these women? Why do they derive so much pleasure from being almost nude in public? Oh, wait. They're not and they don't. We feed our babies as quickly and quietly as possible because *they are hungry* and we don't want their cries *to disturb your very important public business*, such as texting someone while you sip your skinny latte and flick through a newspaper in a coffee shop. Selfish exhibitionists, yes we are.

One time, the week a new–old breastfeeding-in-public media storm broke, I went out to dinner with my family. It was one of those chaotic meals where you end up wearing more food than you eat, cutlery is hurled around, several people burst into tears and you wonder why you didn't all stay home and eat eggs.

Amid the chaos, with the baby squirming madly on my lap and attempting to wear my mushroom pizza as a hat, I whipped out a boob to try to feed him. Or at least, distract him. It was an impulsive move born of equal parts optimism, desperation and defiance.

As I tried in vain to use my body as a human pacifier, there was – for the first time ever – an unspoken challenge in the act. But as usual, nobody seemed to notice. Not that there was much to see. Having almost finished weaning, it was really a blink-and-you'll-miss-'em situation. I did get one withering look, however. From my baby. He was all, 'Oh please, woman, put those pathetic windsocks away. I have so moved on.' To pizza.

His sister was never enamoured with breastfeeding and seemed delighted to give it up so she could devote her full attention to becoming obsessed with pink, princesses, pink princesses and stories about pathetic victims.

Once upon a time there was a grumpy old lady who hated fairytales. In fact, she hated them so much that she would launch into a lively tirade on the subject given the slightest provocation and an audience. This was sometimes boring for those around her and they would roll their eyes behind her back but it made the grumpy lady feel better to vent. The End.

Yes, this is the bah-humbug bit where I tell you how much I'm struggling with Cinderella, Snow White, Rapunzel, Sleeping Beauty and all the other pathetic, insipid, malnourished princess types who have taken up residence all over my house.

They're in doll-form, storybooks, DVDs, the dress-up box and, most worryingly, they're in my daughter's head. All of them. All the time.

The Princess Thing crept into our life insidiously and without warning. One day it was all the harmless innocence of Winnie the Pooh and Dora the Explorer, and the next, we were drowning in a pink sea of Really Bad Messages. Stop rolling your eyes and muttering, 'But they're just *stories*.' I'm serious.

And this is why. Pretty much every mainstream fairytale goes like this: extremely skinny girl gets herself into perilous situation and is desperately unhappy or almost dead before being rescued and redeemed by a handsome prince. There is a wedding and then there is happily ever after.

I know you'll be surprised to hear I have a problem with this blueprint for life. Why don't any of the female characters in fairytales have jobs? Or skills? Or even hobbies? Where are their friends? Why are the 'good' characters always described as beautiful and handsome while the 'bad' characters are always ugly? Why are all step-parents and step-siblings evil? Why does every woman have to be rescued by a prince? Why can't they rescue themselves? And why does a happy ending depend on a wedding and a big white dress? *Why?*

In other words, why doesn't Cinderella go and do a TAFE course to learn a trade other than cleaning, move out

of home and have some therapy to deal with her dysfunctional childhood instead of being such a victim and waiting
around for a fairy godmother and a prince to rock up and
save her with a wand and a wedding?

Not only does this nonsense place unreasonable expectations on men but also on godmothers. And weddings.
Think about it.

It's not just the fairytale messages that horrify me but
also the package they're wrapped in. Have you taken a close
look at animated female characters like Snow White, Sleeping Beauty or Tinkerbell? They are the perfect shape for
little girls to aspire to so long as you don't require any room
for pesky things like internal organs. Oh yes. The princesses
make the models in fashion magazines look morbidly obese.

Despite having been a little girl myself once upon a time,
I don't recall ever being quite so enthralled by all things
princessy. Sure, I watched *The Wonderful World of Disney*
every Sunday night and there were books, but that was all
there was.

But now? Now that pay TV, iPads, smart phones and
DVDs serve up a 24/7 diet of kiddie entertainment, it's far
easier for your child to become obsessed with an aspect of
pop culture and for you to feed that obsession every time

you turn on the TV, leave the house or walk into a shop. In short, you could be forgiven for thinking there is a powerful princess industry designed to infect little girls with fantasies of being saved by Prince Charming and living happily ever after. Because *there is!*

And yet. As I write this, I may as well be wearing a T-shirt with a giant 'HYPOCRITE' written on it (naturally, the T-shirt would be pink and 'hypocrite' would be written with a bedazzler). I have not consistently walked the talk when it comes to my princess misgivings. Instead, I adopt a harm-minimisation approach. This is also called Being Inconsistent And Also A Wussbag.

Currently, there is princess-branded yoghurt in my fridge, princess dolls in the toy box, princess DVDs in the cupboard and princess undies in the wardrobe.

Many of these items were gifts. That's the problem with trying to swim against the tide of pop culture as a parent. There are always gifts. And play-dates at other kids' houses. Unless you live among the Amish or in a Mongolian yurt (don't tempt me), it is impossible to control everything your child is exposed to.

Still, items like the yoghurt *were* bought by me in the desperate hope that a spoonful of princess might make the calcium go down. Wow, I bet the marketers never thought of that!

Overt attempts at bribery aside, my daughter's love affair with these fairytales is so intense that I'm reluctant to deprive her of something that gives her so much joy.

I just wish the narrative wasn't so repetitive and brainwashing. It's scary how many grown women have distorted ideas about relationships that – if you dig a little – come down to a subconscious belief that Prince Charming will someday rock up and save them . . . and *where is he?*

I have no idea. Go ask Cinderella. Or your fairy godmother. My daughter's actual godmother is more suited to the task than anyone I know. While my daughter loses herself in fairytale fantasies of princes and weddings, her godmother has no kids and worships at the temple of Iggy Pop. I am relying on her to sand off a few princess edges and replace them with a more feminist world view.

Thank heavens for women without kids. Not only are they the ideal people to sit next to on planes but they also make excellent sparents.

Throughout history, sparents – spare parents – have played a vital role in the community, taking care of other people's children when their real parents couldn't. And they're still doing it today, albeit not always in such dramatic circumstances.

When it comes to kids, there are three types of women: those who have them, those who don't and those who shouldn't even be around them. It's a pity, then, when Mother Nature gets it wrong. Like when women with the desire and ability to be superb parents can't reproduce due to biology or circumstance, while others who should never be trusted with kids can pop them out more easily than you can spell DoCS.

Darwinism, you're imperfect. And Mother Nature, sometimes you suck.

Among women without children, there are a million personal stories behind their childlessness, and the emotional nuances of these stories range from happiness to pragmatism, relief to devastation. Even ambivalence.

So it's a huge mistake to assume that all women without children are wringing their hands with regret or bitterness. Let's burst that myth right now. Many have made peace with their childlessness and some never even had an internal battle to fight. Like Elizabeth Gilbert, author of mega bestseller *Eat, Pray, Love*.

Elizabeth has no kids and she wants you to know she's fine with that. As she explains, the catalyst for her divorce was her reluctance to have children, something she assumed would be a dealbreaker in any future relationship. Then she met her current husband who was already a dad. His kids are grown and he's done. Kitchen closed. Gas disconnected. And in this they are perfectly matched.

The other myth that proud Aunty Elizabeth is keen to dispel? Childless women are innately selfish. Again, not true. Of her own decision not to have kids, she points out there are many advantages to the community. Childless women have been able to accumulate education and resources they otherwise wouldn't have had if they'd had children. This time and income could then be put back into other people's families 'to pay for lifesaving operations, or to rescue the family farm, or to take in a child whose mother had fallen gravely ill'.

The world is filled with sparents and recent history reflects that. Coco Chanel, John Lennon, Leo Tolstoy, Truman Capote and the Brontë sisters were all raised by their childless aunts. That turned out pretty well.

Thankfully, most sparents aren't required to actually raise anyone else's kids these days. Their role is rarely that drastic. Your average modern sparent is usually just a positive influence, offering a different, less fraught perspective to Mum and Dad. And not every person without children is interested in being a sparent. Many of them are quite content not to play a role in the life of anyone's children and that's fine too.

But if they are interested, the role of a caring, responsible adult in a kid's world should never be underestimated. It's vital.

Sparents are able to dote on your child and connect with them in a way that's often impossible as a parent, particularly as they become teens. This is because your coolness is inversely proportional to the age of your child. The younger they are, the cooler you seem. By the time they hit their teens, you are a walking embarrassment who knows nothing about anything. (FYI, for self-esteem purposes, I highly recommend babies and toddlers, who rate their parents somewhere between Bono and God. With kids of wildly different ages, right now I'm in the unique position of simultaneously being Bono and Bozo the Clown.)

I'm already laying sparental foundations for my children's teenage years, making sure there are plenty of nurturing, responsible adults around to steer them through any issues they don't want to discuss with their embarrassing parents.

My own aunt had her son later in life, which was excellent for me. I was able to benefit from the full force of her love and attention throughout my childhood in a way I wouldn't have been able to do had she had kids earlier. Now a mother herself, she is still a sparent to me and, in a beautiful piece of generational symmetry, her adult son has become a sparent to my own son. Apparently, he is far less embarrassing than me.

A while ago I had dinner with a fabulous single girlfriend who is staring down the barrel of childlessness. She never expected to reach this point but, for whatever reason, the planets have not aligned to make her a mother.

When I asked how she felt about it, she thought for a moment and then she told me about her relationship with her godson. They are incredibly close, have frequent sleepovers and for this little boy, who has two siblings very close in age, my friend is a special source of one-on-one love and attention.

In return, my girlfriend has been able to discover what it feels like to love and nurture a child and to experience the love in return. 'I feel like I have such a connection with him that I've experienced the level of unconditional love parents talk about,' she said, while proudly showing me photos of the little boy on her phone.

There were others at the dinner that night and as we shared calamari entrees, talk turned to someone we knew who was having her fourth round of IVF. 'Has she ever been pregnant before?' I asked. 'No,' came the reply. 'Never.' Oh. There was a brief moment of silence as we sadly contemplated what this meant before someone looked around and asked, 'How many times have you been pregnant?'

There are some questions almost too big to answer. Or too loaded. 'How many times have you been pregnant?' is one of them. It's a question often asked in a medical context (when seeing a new doctor for example), and it's a rare woman who doesn't have to think and blink before she answers. Because for most of us, there are a thousand words and a hundred emotions embedded into the number that hardly ever correlates with the number of children you have. Or don't have.

In the restaurant, as we all looked towards the ceiling in that way you do when you're trying to remember something, we absently started counting on our fingers. Each of us did some quick and intensely personal calculations as our minds travelled back over private moments of joy, dread, devastation, relief, grief, frustration, fear, anger, hope and despair. Among us there were miscarriages, abortions, a still-birth . . . In other words, we were a typical group of women in our thirties and forties.

A woman's gynaecological history is fertile ground for complex emotions and many, many anecdotes that are rarely shared except among close girlfriends. But once you turn on the tap . . .

Someone ordered another bottle of wine as we remembered all the pregnancies we'd lost. This sounds terribly maudlin but it was in fact cathartic and natural, particularly for those of us who had children. Such conversations are far more poignant and painful for those who don't.

Between the five of us, we counted nine children and twenty-seven pregnancies. It took a while to do the numbers because each one had a story attached although, admittedly, for the mother who'd had nine miscarriages in five years, they blurred a little. I'm writing about this because pregnancy loss remains one of the big secrets of motherhood – actually it's one of the biggest secrets of women's lives.

I had two miscarriages. Because the first one was late in

my pregnancy and I had a media profile at the time, it was an uncomfortably public experience. As difficult as that was to endure, there were some benefits to people knowing what had happened without me having to explain.

Through the fog of my grief, I discovered that pregnancy loss is like a secret society you never asked to join. So many women describe it that way. You don't realise how many members there are until you become one of them.

'Oh, it happened to me last year, it's so hard,' said a colleague, squeezing my arm. 'I had four miscarriages with IVF before I finally had my twins,' confessed the woman at the coffee shop, slipping me a free biscotti. 'My sister had a miscarriage before each of her kids,' confided a girlfriend, giving me a hug. 'Dear, you know my son had a twin brother but he died before he was born,' whispered an elderly relative, patting my hand.

In their heartfelt efforts to console you, the private stories of other women bubble up and make you feel a little less alone. Because miscarriage can be a lonely journey and an odd type of grief, mourning someone you never met. In many ways you're grieving an imagined future.

We're very good at celebrating good news in our culture. You're pregnant! Engaged! You got married! Had a baby!

Bought a house! Got a promotion! But we're collectively hopeless when it comes to acknowledging things that are painful, awkward, unpleasant and sad. Things like pregnancy loss. It's not that people don't mean well when they say things like 'Oh well, it's nature's way' and 'Better it happened early rather than later' and 'At least you have a child already. Count your blessings!' There's truth in all those platitudes, but in our hurry to make someone look at the silver lining, we often overlook their need to acknowledge the cloud.

There's a Japanese tradition called *mizuko kuyo*, which translates literally as 'foetus memorial service' and it's a ceremony for those who have had a miscarriage, stillbirth or termination. The practice has gained popularity since the 1970s and, as the *New York Times* reports, temple worshipers pay a fee to 'adopt' a small stone statue called a *mizuko* and inscribe their names on it. 'They often regard it as representing their own lost baby and they dress up the *mizuko* figurines like little newborns, wrapping them with bibs, hand-knit sweaters, booties or hats against the cold. And they pour water over the childlike figurines to quench their thirst.' To some, this might sound comical but if you've ever grieved for a baby you never had a chance to meet, you'll recognise the deep poignancy of having a place to go and mourn. In our culture there are no rituals for miscarriage and that's such a shame.

So if you're a member of that secret society none of us ever wanted to join, either now or in the future, know this: you're not alone.

Whatever

Job interviews have changed. I didn't realise this until I had to recruit an employee for the first time in years and found myself doing some surprising things. When I worked in magazines, I disliked hiring even more than firing. And this was problematic because when you spend a decade managing women in their twenties and thirties who bounce around between jobs, countries and babies, you want to be friends with recruitment.

Résumés? I've seen a few. Million.

Very occasionally in a job interview, magic happens. I've experienced it three times in my career, and each time, not only did the job work out beautifully but the person on the other side of the desk also became a close friend.

My first taste of magic happened in the first proper job interview I ever went to. I was nineteen and I'd been fortunate enough to score an opportunity to meet with *Cleo* editor Lisa Wilkinson about a work-experience placement.

Well, it was certainly magic for me. Actually? It was love. I was star-struck almost to the point of muteness to be in such close proximity to my idol and, almost twenty years later, I still remember every detail of that twenty-minute meeting. She had me at hello and it only took me six months of persistent nagging to secure an actual job with a pay cheque.

Years later when I was an editor myself, interviewing new staff quickly shot to the top of my Things I Loathe list. I don't know many employers who enjoy recruitment. It's a hideous combination of time consuming, awkward, tedious and risky. The cost of making the wrong decision is high, particularly since it can lead to yet more recruitment. But you persevere in the hope of magic. Or at least competence.

One dull day, while interviewing for a new PA, a tall girl with an enormous smile bounded into my office and, for the second time in an interview, it was love at first sight. Magic. Ten years later, and that office now belongs to her.

After hiring Bron as my PA, she went on to land my job,

just as I'd always known she would. And just like with Lisa, Bron and I went on to become close friends, our families intertwined to this day.

A few years after hiring Bron, I was looking to fill another empty junior chair. In fact, it was Bron's chair because she was moving from her role as Beauty Editor to more senior editorial pastures. Drowning in a boring sea of CVs, demoralised by their mind-numbing sameness, suddenly, like a shining beacon, I glimpsed the name 'Rupert Murdoch' and a signature.

When you're hiring from a pool of 22-year-olds, that's unusual. On closer inspection it was a written reference from Mr Murdoch, raving about the talent and brilliance of a certain witty young writer. Except it wasn't from Rupert, it was by the writer herself and for the first time ever while reading a CV, I laughed out loud. I knew I had to meet this girl, and for the third time, there was interview magic. I hired her immediately, she impressed me every day and I've watched Zoe's stellar rise as a writer and author like the proud friend I have become.

I also hired dozens of perfectly terrific staff over the years, as well as some who proved to be massive disappointments and many who were utterly forgettable. And all those hours and days and years and lifetimes I spent sifting through CVs and smiling and nodding through interviews? I will never get them back.

So yes, one of the best things about leaving behind my life as a manager in a big company was no more recruitment. But as Mamamia.com.au continued to grow, and after several years of doing everything myself, I was finally forced to wave the white flag and admit it was time to hire a PA/site co-ordinator.

I didn't have time to trawl through a thousand résumés, nor did I have the stomach to disappoint 999 hopefuls. I was too busy and impatient. Basically, I needed an assistant to help me find an assistant. Since that wasn't logically possible, I instead asked around my media contacts and edited their leads down to five good prospects.

That's when it became interesting. Have I mentioned I find CVs useless? Mostly because they're the work equivalent of the profiles people post on dating sites: 100 per cent spin.

Without even consciously thinking about it, the first thing I did before meeting each candidate was to look them up on Facebook and Twitter.

Interesting . . .

And then there were two.

Much to the horror of many people who will be reading this, I eliminated three girls based on their social-media profiles alone. Oh yes I did and here's why. One girl had a constant stream of Facebook updates bitching indiscreetly about her current job and boss. Another evidently spent much of her time proudly obliterating herself with drugs and alcohol, and a third had some strident views, if by 'strident' you mean racist.

Was this fair? Sensible? Justified? Who knows, but I did it. I made judgements on the character of job applicants based on their social-media profiles.

And why wouldn't I? It's the modern equivalent of 'asking around' or checking character references. How else can you find out a bit about the type of person you're hiring? By calling their mother?

It is absurd to believe that how you behave on social-media sites can be quarantined from your 'proper' work life. It can't.

Soon after being elected president of the United States, Barack Obama spoke to a group of high school kids. Asked by one student how he could become president someday, Obama had this to say: 'I want everybody here to be careful about what you post on Facebook, because in the YouTube age, whatever you do, it will be pulled up again later somewhere in your life. That's number one.'

And I'm going to go out on a limb here and suggest that parts two, three and four of Obama's advice are irrelevant if a simple Google search of your name reveals photos of you flashing your boobs, as well as the fact that you're a member of a Facebook group called 'F*** off foreigners, we're full!'

See? I'm in good company here. Me and Obama, both of us emphasising that what you put on your social-media page today may be something you regret tomorrow – to the power of a thousand when it comes to job interviews or a future political career.

Think of your social-media profiles as being like your shop window. It's not your bedroom. It's not private. And it can also become your digital fingerprint, a better indication of character than any written reference. And just like fingerprints, it leaves traces.

When I first wrote about how I look at social-media profiles as part of my recruitment process, many people were horrified. I was accused of 'stalking' job applicants. Of 'hacking' into private Facebook accounts. (I was a little bit chuffed that anyone would think I had the technical know-how to do such a thing.) And of 'practically hiring a private investigator'.

Not quite.

There was a surprising amount of indignation that something as 'personal' as a Facebook profile could cruel someone's chances of a job, as if somehow this was my fault. But here's the thing: the relationship between an employer and a prospective employee is not equal. Let's not pretend it is. There are many reasons why someone does or doesn't get a job and not all of them can be laid out in a spreadsheet. Some of it *is* personal. Otherwise you could hire a computer. Or a transformer.

When you are hiring a person to represent your company (or yourself), character matters.

And if you have a problem with that, you'd better take a long hard look at your social-media privacy settings.

So anyway. One of the girls I trialled was great. Until we got to the end of the fortnight when she announced she was 'confused' and didn't know what she wanted to do with her career and perhaps magazines were more her thing. So, in essence, she sacked me before she got the job. Terrific. Then I found an old email from someone who wanted to do some work experience. We met. I hired her. She's fabulous. And I still haven't checked her Facebook page.

See, I told you recruitment was stressful. Almost more stressful than not having anyone to help me with work. I'm not terribly effective when I'm overwhelmed by stress, mostly because I don't have many ways to alleviate it.

Exercise helps. So does shopping for things I don't need and which I'll invariably return. But that's more of a distraction than an effective form of stress release.

Generally, I find forced relaxation to be very stressful. Which is a drag really since I could benefit from some Zen. Even when I'm not stressed, I'm someone who likes to be busy. Fond of multi-tasking. Best when juggling a number of different things, despite the fact I may be dropping balls all over the floor.

Because my mind is so rubbish at being idle, one of the most challenging activities for me is having a massage. Yes, I know. The words 'massage' and 'challenging' are not natural companions, except in the case of odd balls like me who find it exceptionally difficult to take a chill pill. Many of my friends swear by massages but, as hard as I've tried over the years, they're just not my thing.

One time, as a treat, I took myself off for a few days to Gwinganna Lifestyle Retreat where I had a number of lovely massages, all of which I managed to turn into opportunities to feel tense.

First up was a ninety-minute remedial massage in the tranquil haven of the retreat's Spa Sanctuary. As I changed into the fluffy white robe I'd been given and listened to the peaceful bird noises in the surrounding bush, I had that familiar moment of angst: undies on or undies off?

Now, despite the fact I've had dozens of massages in my life, I can never *ever* remember the protocol. Both options seem fraught if you get it wrong. Take your knickers off when you're meant to leave them on? You're a pervert. Leave them on when you're meant to be naked? You're a prude. And inherent in each choice is the risk of having to have a conversation with a stranger about your underpants, which I am always desperately keen to avoid.

Alone in the change room, I stood frozen for a few moments, paralysed by the weight of making the wrong decision. 'Oh, stop being ridiculous,' I chastised myself eventually. 'Just take them off.' So I did.

Feeling airy and liberated under my robe, I sat in the lounge area and sipped some calming tea as I waited for my massage therapist to come and get me. Silently, and seemingly from nowhere, a very tall and good-looking guy appeared. He had an interesting configuration of facial hair somewhere between a goatee and stubble and he smiled serenely at me.

'Hi, Mia, I'm Josh and I'll be doing your massage today.'

Pause.

'Uh, Josh? I'll be right back!'

Safely ensconced back in my knickers, I spent the next ninety minutes trying valiantly to relax while an attractive stranger worked his magic on my tense muscles. I'm pretty sure they were tense even before the underpants incident but it didn't help.

Even when I have a massage with a female therapist, I still find ways to be uptight.

Sometimes, lying with my face in the massage table, my nose gets all blocked and I become distracted by whether to keep sniffing or to ask for a tissue. 'But what if she thinks I have a cold?' I fret inexplicably while another more sane part of my mind shouts, 'Shut up and enjoy this while it lasts, you angsty fool!'

My natural state is mute and powerless during a massage, even though I am a paying customer and even though every therapist tells you to speak up if you're too hot or too cold, if their pressure is too hard or too soft, or if you wish to alter any of a hundred variable environmental conditions.

I never ask for anything and I have no idea why this is. Because I don't want to sound like a whinger? Because I feel like they're going to enough trouble already? Because I'm still thinking about my underpants?

Once I did ask for something and it didn't go well.

A couple of years ago, faced with a particularly ugly book deadline, I went to another health spa, hoping to churn out a good chunk of work in a quiet, solitary place without kids or distractions.

On the second day I booked a massage, and as the therapist showed me where to put my clothes and fired up the aromatherapy burner, I cleared my throat awkwardly.

'Um, I know this is a really weird question,' I said in a voice that sounded way too loud in the small room, 'but is there a powerpoint I could use to recharge my laptop during the massage?'

She looked at me as if I had just said, 'Would it be okay if I rack up a few lines of cocaine and snort them off a hooker's ass before we get started?'

Plink-plinkity-plink-plink went the sound of the waterfall

music playing softly in the background as she considered my request, frowning. 'Um, you could plug it in just over there, I guess.'

Feeling the sting of her disapproval, I tried to make light of the situation. 'Haha! It's just that I need to use it afterwards and the battery is dead. I promise I won't be checking my emails or anything during the treatment! Hahaha!'

Silence. Not even a polite laugh. O-kaaaaay then. Naturally, I spent the rest of that massage feeling awkward, tense and disapproved of. Are you noticing a pattern here? And don't even get me started on facials . . .

Surely I'm not the only one who loses my assertiveness when faced with someone touching me. Am I?

I have a friend who is worse and I'm reminded of this every time I meet her after she's been to the hairdresser. Invariably, she's late. This is not because her hairdresser runs over time. It is because after having her hair cut, coloured and blow dried, she goes *home to wash it and dry it again!*

'You are nuts, you know that, don't you?' I told her one day, as she sat down at our table in the café thirty-five minutes after our agreed meeting time. 'I cannot believe you still go to that hairdresser.'

My friend had the decency to look part sheepish, part wretched. 'I know, I know,' she grimaced. 'I'm hopeless.'

How did this happen? How did this intelligent, assertive woman end up trapped in such a dysfunctional relationship with her hairdresser? As the customer in this transaction, how did she surrender her power and lose her voice? She's not sure. All she knows is that she's been going to the same salon for ten years and has her hair cut the same way by the same guy. She likes him. She likes the way he cuts and colours her hair.

What she hates is the blow dry afterwards because he does this flicky thing that makes her look like a newsreader circa 1994. But instead of asking him to do it differently, she sucks up her flicks, thanks him profusely and then dashes home to wash out 1994. She then blow dries it again from scratch before resuming her day, or what little is left of it. My friend has been doing this for years and barely questions it any more. I, however, question it. Often. I think it's mental and never miss an opportunity to tell her so.

'I don't want to talk about it,' she insists whenever I bring it up. 'I know, it's stupid and I'm an idiot.' I nod. She continues. 'I have no rational explanation for why I can't ask him to dry my hair the way I want it. But it's too late for that. I had my chance years ago and I chickened out and now I'm trapped. Window closed. The end. Shall we have a glass of wine?'

If it were just one friend who did something like this, I'd dismiss it as a quirk. But virtually every woman I know has, at some point, found herself trapped in a dysfunctional relationship with a service provider. Including me.

Some of these relationships are long-term, like a hairdresser, a cleaner or a doctor, while others are casually dysfunctional.

Like my friend who will drink the wrong coffee because she can't tell the barista he stuffed up her order. 'I never say anything,' she admits, despite skillfully managing a staff of twelve. 'Even if it means drinking one of those soy monstrosities that taste like bong water.'

Another friend is perfectly able to complain about her $4 coffee but charge her $80 for a massage and she becomes mute. 'If the masseuse starts chatting, I never ask her to be quiet no matter how much I hate it. I just lie there feeling tense. I even chat back to be polite. Then at the end of it I pay my money and feel totally stressed and ripped off. But next time it's the same. Why can't I just say, "Would you mind if I didn't talk?" Maybe it's the vulnerability of lying there in my knickers.'

Yes. Knickers. The more intimate and personal the service, the more difficult it can be to assert yourself. If someone is touching a part of your body, it's awkward to tell them you don't like their work, isn't it?

'Last month I had my eyebrows waxed and along with a few stray hairs the beautician also waxed off half my face,' grumbles another friend. 'I had red, raw, scabby eyebrows for a week because she ripped off so much skin with her too-hot wax. Instead of complaining and refusing to pay, I told the girl it was fine and that it didn't hurt at all. I paid my thirty bucks and walked out nursing my shredded face. Wait, it gets worse. I even made a follow-up appointment for six weeks time. I'm ashamed.'

Without exception, the women I know who roll over like this (and it is mostly women) have no trouble being assertive in most situations. None of us could ever be described as doormats. We are positively bolshie as employees, bosses, partners, mothers, daughters, sisters and friends. But in particular circumstances as customers, our assertiveness evaporates and we end up swallowing our frustration and dissatisfaction for the sake of . . . what exactly? A need to be liked? A fear of confrontation?

'There's almost an embarrassment I feel when something

goes wrong or isn't delivered the way I expected,' theorises the friend with the wax burns. 'Instead of standing up for myself and asking for a refund I smile and pretend *great! That's exactly what I wanted* . . . and then I run away, cursing silently.'

'I think it's that we don't want to offend people to their face,' says a different friend who wants to change doctors but is too embarrassed to ask for her medical records. 'Saying you don't like a haircut or telling your cleaner that the house is still filthy is basically like saying, "Hey, you know your chosen career? Well, you're crap at it." It's awkward for all involved.'

You bet. It's far less awkward to pay money to have your hair looking ridiculous, your face stripped of skin or your shoulders in tension knots after a massage . . .

I wonder if this reluctance to speak up when we're displeased has something to do with it being a face-to-face confrontation. We have so few of those any more. I do virtually all of my confronting electronically, via email or text.

Worryingly, I fear this is yet more proof that I'm losing my social skills. The evidence is mounting and it's becoming hard to ignore. Consider this: I prefer emails and texts to voices (particularly when it comes to confrontation, see above). My mobile is always switched to silent. When my home phone rings, my reaction is usually 'startled' followed by 'irritated'. My distaste for small talk has escalated to the point where I'd prefer to stay home with my laptop than have to make meaningless chitchat with strangers.

On the downside, for those of us who love texting and Twitter and email, we're losing the ability to prioritise our communication. Technology is a pushy, queue-jumping little bugger. It's easy to confuse immediacy with importance, which is why I will answer an email in the middle of writing a column. Or reply to a stupid text in the middle of a wonderful dinner with girlfriends I haven't seen in months.

Real communication – face-to-face or voice-to-voice – is messy and that's what makes it wonderful. It's spontaneous and unpredictable. You can't control it. You can't abruptly terminate it when you've had enough and you can't be sure that someone will let you finish what you want to say. Electronic communication, while cleaner, can also be narcissistic. In writing, nobody can interrupt you. Maybe *that's* why I like it so much.

From an early age I've preferred to communicate in writing. Instead of throwing tantrums as a kid, I used to write notes to whichever member of my family had cheesed me off, explaining in detail why I didn't like them, why my life wasn't fair and why I'd decided to run away from home. I never did actually run away. The act of writing down my feelings somehow diffused them and I'd wander off to the kitchen to make myself some honey toast instead.

And perhaps this is exactly why I'm drawn to writing. For me, the act of committing words to paper or a screen helps me to organise my thoughts and articulate them more clearly. In conversations I can ramble, and so more and more over the years, I find myself eschewing talking for typing or texting.

When you're feeling time poor, electronic communication is your friend. Texts don't encourage tangents. Or verbosity.

I tried to explain this to my son when he asked why I didn't call a friend instead of texting her. 'I don't have *time*,' I sighed as he looked at me, puzzled.

'But why can't you just say, "Hi, do you want to go out for dinner on Saturday night?" and they'll answer and then you say goodbye and hang up.'

Ah, youth. Male youth.

'Look, it's just not possible to have such a basic conversation when you're female,' I explained. 'If I call, I'll be forced to chat, and ask and answer questions for twenty minutes *at least*, which would be fine at another time BUT NOT NOW WHEN MUMMY IS ON DEADLINE. Okay?'

It's not that I don't like people. I do. I like people very much. My girlfriends and my family are my lifeblood. Even people I don't know fascinate me. I'm innately curious about everyone. It's just that I often find electronic communication easier. Faster. More efficient.

Part of this is a gender thing. One of the best yet most challenging aspects of being female is having the ability to mentally multi-task within a single conversation. This is both nifty and exhausting. It's also a time-sucker because it leads to lengthy phone conversations as you dart about the place, jumping from subject to subject with endless tangents. Socially, this is the only type of phone call many women are capable of.

I don't think I've ever spoken to a girlfriend on the phone for less than ten minutes in my life unless we've been cut off. And in that time we will barely skim the surface. There's just so much to catch up on. Her life, my life, our jobs, kids, partners, gossip about people we will never meet, future plans to catch-up . . . the list of subjects to cover is endless. And to skip any of them would seem plain rude, ruder than not calling at all.

Modern communication is built on a foundation of control. We want to trade information but only on our terms. We don't want to have to make small talk with anyone other than the object of our call and frequently not even them.

One friend who works in PR explains it this way: 'I find my job is so "talky" that I would rather cut the chitchat and just do a pure information transaction with my friends. I can't stand the waffling on the phone. I just want to know times, places and so on. And when I was dating I couldn't stand guys who called all the time. I just wanted to text.'

Whatever your communication personality, be sure of this: all other communication personalities will piss you off. Recently, I was hassling a friend about never returning texts. He mounted a counter-attack, accusing me of never answering my phone. True.

Here's another weird thing: I've become increasingly reluctant to ambush my friends with unannounced phone calls. Lately, I find myself texting them first to flag that I'll be calling. I do this so they're prepared when they hear my voice. Prepared for what is unclear. It's not like I'm about to announce I'm breaking up with them and moving to Hong Kong.

Still, it doesn't always work because no one takes calls

any more. We just return them. Have you noticed? Making contact with someone these days is enough to send you reaching for the Rescue Remedy and a bank loan. First, you ring someone and it invariably goes through to their voicemail. Ka-ching! Then they have to access their message bank to hear your message. Ka-ching! Then they call you back and get your voicemail. Ka-ching! Then you access your message bank to hear their message. Ka-ching! So far, that's four different charges paid to a telco without a single word having been exchanged in real time.

Of course, if you're both female, this will be no impediment to your friendship. Hell no. I have several friends with whom I can go months on voicemail messages alone, leaving each other a series of sequential monologues. They are detailed, animated and very, very long. In said monologues, we update each other on our life, ask each other questions and answer questions from previous monologues. Sometimes we ask ourselves questions and then answer them.

Many women do this. We are virtually incapable of leaving a man-style message, which usually involves one subject, one verb and one object. As in: 'Mate, call me.' Can you imagine?

Two weeks ago I was driving home from work and

listening to my messages on hands-free. One girlfriend's message started at the beginning of my journey and didn't finish until I had driven a good 5 kilometres in traffic. Eight minutes later. This is not unusual. For the past few months we have been leaving each other elaborate soliloquies, like a conversation but with only one side. I struggle to recall our last real-time conversation but I still feel totally up-to-date with her life and headspace.

At the other extreme of the communication scale, there are parties. That's when you are forced to communicate, in person with many, many people at once, while simultaneously balancing a glass of alcohol and something small and unsatisfying to eat, all while teetering on high heels and trying to lubricate yourself between bursts of small talk with people you don't know very well.

Are we having fun yet?

Partying is not a skill on my social CV.

Frequently, I suffer from an affliction called Party PMT. I'm not sure if this condition is recognised by health authorities because I just made it up, but it's the only way to describe my behaviour.

Party PMT is much like the menstrual kind but with

canapés and a DJ. Symptoms include stroppiness, sulking, immaturity, extreme petulance and a type of Tourette's syndrome where you're powerless to stop the words coming out of your mouth. Words like 'I hate this party. I hate everyone here. I hate my outfit. I'm hungry. I'm tired. I'm too hot. I'm too cold. I'm too old. I'm over it. I want to go home.'

Party PMT can be triggered by many things (including PMT itself), but one common cause is a bad choice of outfit. Shallow, yes, but it's a girl thing. I'm yet to meet a man whose night was ruined by the pants he wished he hadn't worn.

Another cause is being on a different, er, wavelength to the majority of your fellow guests, i.e. they're wired or wasted and you're not. Being around drunk people can be hard. Especially if they're sleazy, loud or vomiting. But being around people who are wired on drugs can be even more excruciating because they invariably want to talk to you. A lot.

A typical conversation goes like this:

Wired: 'OHMYGOD, how ARE you? You look amaaazing! Isn't this just THE BEST party? Are you having THE BEST time? I sooo am. This is like THE MOST

AMAZING night. God, I love your outfit! Where's it from? And your shoes are just SO FANTASTIC.'

Straight: 'Oh, thanks.'

Wired: 'You know, I've always wanted to tell you that I think you're such a great person! I know we don't know each other very well, or actually at all, but I've always thought we'd make UNREAL friends because we're just so alike and so, you know, it would be BRILLIANT if we had, like, coffee or lunch or something, and caught up properly, don't you think? Like, so we can really talk! What's your mobile and I'll call you tomorrow morning and we can arrange it for maybe tomorrow even! Or the day after! But you have to swear that you won't forget this conversation, okay? I've just got to nick to the bathroom quickly but I'll be right back and let's talk lots more, okay? Promise you won't go anywhere? You have to promise. God, this is a FABULOUS party. Stay right there. I'll be two seconds. Your shoes are SO GREAT!'

My worst case of Party PMT was New Year's Eve several years ago. I was a disgrace. I'd been invited to a spectacular party. Harbourside. Incredible house. Gun-barrel view of the fireworks. Abundant food and cocktails. Gracious and generous hosts. A hot mix of funky, fashionable and famous guests. The late Heath Ledger was DJ-ing, although I didn't see much of him because I sat on a bench under a tree all night sulking and texting people about how miserable I was. Wasn't my husband lucky to have such a fun date?

I maintain that a large part of my sulk was justified because I did, in fact, have on the wrong outfit. Not just a little bit wrong, like the difference between 'black tie' and 'lounge suit' (which is negligible). Oh no. My husband had forgotten to tell me that it was a fancy-dress party. The theme? Rock Star Glamour. My outfit? A sundress and thongs. Surrounded by guests who were fabulously OTT with their costumes (think sequins, sunnies, leather, lycra, hotpants, micro-minis, platforms and the like), I felt like someone's dowdy spinster aunty in my cotton frock. And despite reaching for the cocktails in a bid to manufacture some festive spirit, Party PMT played its trump card: alcohol immunity. Three cocktails and not even a mild buzz. At midnight, as the fireworks exploded and everyone started hugging and kissing, I found myself trying to pick a fight with my husband about whether the fireworks budget should have been donated to charity. When one Rock Star Glamour couple spontaneously got engaged and I began muttering darkly about breath-testing, I knew it was time to call it a night and a disaster in that order.

I have a theory about flowers that also applies to diamond rings. My flower theory goes that the man who sends flowers to a woman at her workplace wins more points than the man who presents them privately. Because it's not just about the flowers, it's about other people *seeing* the flowers. And so it is with some women and their diamonds.

During the years I worked in an office full of women, I watched many of them bounce in to announce their engagements. What happened next was predictable. A crowd would form instantly and, as one, they'd chorus, 'Let's see the ring!' This was never necessary because the girl's left hand would already be thrust out in front of her. There would be squeals. Gushing. But the future groom's name was rarely mentioned. Even the proposal story was secondary to the examination and discussion of the Ring.

Occasionally, like at that New Year's Eve party, when a nervous, spontaneous (or drunk) man decided the pressure of choosing such a significant and expensive item alone was too great, there would be no ring. When that happened, the crowd dissipated quickly. The collective disappointment was palpable, the anti-climax acute. No ring? No squeals. I always found this ritual boring and cringey. It made me uncomfortable the way some girls focused on the ring instead of the engagement – and they're usually the same ones who focus on the wedding instead of the marriage.

Because, really, what's love got to do with money, status or rings? This is a genuine question.

You see, unlike almost every other woman I know, I don't speak diamond or any other jewellery language. I do wear a diamond ring but I cannot tell you a thing about it because I don't know any ring words. Well, maybe I know a few, gleaned by osmosis during the microseconds between when someone starts speaking about their ring and I start thinking about . . . oh, anything. But even those words are useless because I don't know what they mean. I can't tell you what a carat is, or a princess cut or a solitaire. Speak to me of settings or stones and my eyes will glaze over. Clarity? I have none. I do know that rubies are red but that's only because of the rhyme (violets are blue etc.).

I'm unsure how I managed to avoid learning this essential information. Who was meant to teach me? School? My mum? She doesn't speak diamond either so no luck there. The consequence of this ignorance is that I've never understood the fuss over diamonds or jewellery. The sound you just heard is my husband high-fiving himself while other men mutter, 'Lucky bastard!'

Long before he proposed, I made a pre-emptive strike, presumptuously announcing I didn't want a diamond. 'I think flashy engagement rings are cheesy,' I insisted, although I didn't mean cheesy exactly. I meant I didn't need a big rock on my finger to feel loved or to impress anyone.

Several years after we married, I changed my mind. To my surprise, I wanted a diamond ring. Apart from being prone to both hypocrisy and inconsistency, my reasons were simple. One? I'm a sheep and the tradition of it is nice. Two? I like sparkly things. It was that basic. I still cared not a jot about cut or colour or clarity or cash outlay. It could have been a piece of glass. I just wanted a sparkly ring. Another victory for the diamond marketers.

And now that they've conquered me? Their next conquest is single women. Determined to exploit every possible market, the new push from the diamond industry is 'the Right Hand Ring', a way for single women of independent means to 'empower' themselves by buying their own diamond! Or, to paraphrase Beyoncé, all the single ladies, go put a ring on it yourself. It's a diamond-as-feminist statement. Go figure.

The trend has already trickled down to the street with fashion chainstores selling pretend diamond rings to young girls for $9.95.

Of course, there are some women who really can be bought with diamonds. Like the one I know who discovered her husband had done some inappropriate things with a stripper at a bucks party. 'Are you okay?' inquired one of her friends, worriedly. 'I'm devastated,' she replied. 'But I've chosen some diamond earrings and he's bringing them home tonight. They'll help.'

I do believe that's called a Faustian bargain. But Faust has nothing to do with another bargain made by many women when they marry.

Here comes the bride and there goes her name. I've lost count of the number of emails I've received that go something like this: 'Please note that my name has changed to Louise Taylor. My new email address is below so you can update your contacts.' Fortunately, most of us now keep our address books in electronic form rather than paper; otherwise they'd be a crossed-out mess.

I can name seven newly married friends and colleagues who have changed their name in the recent past. Well, I can name the ones whose new surname I remember. Several, I don't. I've begun alphabetising all my contacts by their first name for this reason.

Once upon a time, I would have been surprised, even slightly disappointed, that so many women were giving up their identities to take on their husband's name. Now I barely notice let alone feel the sting of disapproval. It seems the feminist debate has moved on.

'My first name is my identity,' points out a married colleague who changed her name a few years ago. 'My maiden name is my father's surname. Changing it is symbolic because it signifies the shift from my family of origin – my parents – to my family of creation – my husband and our son.'

There was a brief window in our social history when it was popular for married women to keep their maiden name. Those women are mostly in their forties now, sandwiched between an older generation who didn't dare challenge the marital status quo and a younger generation who has nothing to prove.

For some women who kept their name, it was a feminist issue. They resented any connotation of ownership by their new husband; their name was their identity. For others it was practical. They'd built a reputation and a career on the back of their name and didn't want to lose that equity.

With some exceptions, naturally, today's newlyweds see things differently. For a generation to whom the word 'feminism' has become a pejorative and the word 'housewife' has become a campy, ironic badge of honour, changing your name doesn't even rate on the angst scale. 'It's just not a feminist issue – are there even any of those left any more?' asks my friend Amanda wryly after changing her name. 'Didn't we get what we wanted and decide we didn't want most of it anyway?'

I was discussing this with a woman in her early fifties recently and she was horrified to hear that young women were abandoning their surname without a backwards glance. I explained that women just didn't view taking their husband's name as disempowering. 'Of course they don't,' she sighed. 'That's because they've never had to fight for anything. Men would never change their name,' she added. 'Why are women so quick to give up theirs?'

Perhaps it's not a feminist issue; it's a makeover issue. Women simply like to re-invent. Changing your name can be a bit like having your hair cut after a break-up: new chapter, new me.

'I wasn't going to change but at the last minute I got swept away with the romance and decided to,' a career-minded thirty-year-old friend explains. 'Plus, everyone assumed I wouldn't – you know, work reputation etc. – but let's face it, I wasn't the president and one email was all that was required to make it happen at work. Then I just did the rounds of the RTA, my bank and Medicare with my marriage certificate, got everything replaced for free and made up a new signature. It was quite fun actually; like a fresh start.'

So what do the blokes make of all this? Do they even care? 'My husband had no say in it at all,' insists one friend, who adds, 'He didn't really mind either way – just as long as he didn't have to wear a ring, which was fine by me.'

Another friend's husband took a thoroughly modern approach: 'He said that it was a big move to change names, and if I was prepared to hyphenate, he would too. Lots of brownie points there. I did consider it but Stefanopolous-Patterson wouldn't fit on a credit card so I ditched my name and took his. That's the only reason. How romantic of me!'

The last word goes to my friend Amanda who had second thoughts about her new name. 'I wanted to change mine back about a year after we were married and asked Brendan if he'd mind. He said, "How would you do that?"

I said, "Easy – just send an email around." He said, "Why don't you just send one that says now that the wedding is over and you're no longer a bride, you need some attention instead?" We didn't discuss it again.'

I'm predicting that the next generation is going to be keener to change their first name rather than their surname.

I'm not talking about the little boy called Notorious or his sister Awesome. Nor am I talking about Chanel or Bongo or Stalin or Mars, even though all those kids exist.

I'm referring to Sindi. And Kymberleigh. And Lyriq and Xal (pronounced Crystal) and Paege and Beeanchor (say it out loud, you'll get it eventually) and Jazz-man and Ararh-bella and Sumher. It's also about Jamze, Taiylah, Khrystie, Jesinta, Naithon, Madisonne and Mersaydeez.

I'm talking about what happens when the alphabet vomits on a birth certificate. It's about wacky spellings and the parents who inflict them on their children.

The patron saint of trickily spelled names may be *Kath & Kim*'s Epponnee-Rae but tricky spelling is not a new phenomenon. And we know this because the first generation afflicted by it is coming of age.

Whenever I do book signings, I have to be very careful to

get the spelling of someone's name right, lest I stuff up the copy of the book they've just bought (bless them). You must never take a name for granted. 'Hello, Anna, nice to meet you!' I say. 'And how do you spell Anna?' Seriously. Because these days, it could also be Annah, Ana or Anar.

I once read about a girl called Kyly. Yes, Kyly. When I remarked upon the strangeness of this, someone I know called Kylie wondered, 'What did her parents have against vowels?'

Having inquired among those who know trickily spelled people and those who named them, my suspicions have been confirmed. It's not about vowel discrimination (Tylr) or a love of silent letters (Tcharli) or phonetics (Moneeke). The root of tricky spelling is a desire to be different. Special. Unique. Which is fine on a birth certificate but more challenging in the real world where people communicate verbally.

My parents named me Mia for a number of reasons, chief among them that they weren't fans of nicknames and thought Mia wouldn't be shortened. They were right about that, but what they didn't factor in was that many people are stupid. You'd think a name with three letters that is pronounced phonetically wouldn't pose too many problems but you'd be so wrong.

For years my name has mistakenly been pronounced

'My-a' or spelled incorrectly. In fact whenever someone has to write my name down, I automatically launch into 'Mia – M-I-A', before going on to spell my surname.

One day, I asked the name of a salesperson I was speaking to on the phone and she replied, 'Mia – M-I-A,' so it appears it's not just me.

I'm telling you this because if my simple name is going to cause problems, what hope is there for poor Beeanchor? How many years of her life will she waste explaining, 'It's BIANCA – yes, I know it's unusual to spell it like that.' A burdensome number. And will it make her feel special? Or will it just make her parents feel clever?

Here's a clue: any name that requires you to add 'pronounced . . .' after it is an undue burden to place on another human being.

I asked on Twitter about tricky spellings and got some doozies. One person involved in family law said, 'The best names I've seen through my work are La-a (pronounced Ladasha), Abcde (Ab-se-dee) and the very popular Nevaeh (Heaven backwards).' Someone who worked in a maternity ward told me the staff keeps a running list of the weirdest names. Current winner: N-ah (Nadasha). No doubt the sister of La-a.

Stop it. I'm calling DoCS.

But *why* do they do it? Often the reasons are quite specific. 'My friend named her daughter Olyvia because her name is Melyssa,' said one woman. I also heard from the creatively spelled themselves. Like Rihannon. 'It's meant to be Rhiannon but my dad made a spelling mistake on my birth certificate. I'm now forever correcting people.' And Tiffiny. 'I hate it! I never get my emails and all because Mum didn't want me nicknamed Fany.'

Then there are traditional spellings like the Irish name Aoibhe (pronounced Ava) and the Celtic name Niamh (pronounced Neev). Good luck with that.

Generally, though, it was agreed by everyone that the most common reason for tricky spelling is a desire for your child to stand out from the crowd.

In looking into alphabetical vomit, I stumbled upon a forum on a baby names site that had the following question from a pregnant woman: 'I love the name Chloe but I don't like the spelling. I love changing spelling around . . . Is there anyone that thinks that Khloei is just too weird of a change? And for a boy or girl the name Aiden changing to Aydyn?'

The response was fairly rigorous and unanimously negative. As one person said, 'I'm not opposed to spelling variations within reason (Alan/Allen Catherine/Katherine) but completely invented spellings are not my thing.'

I wanted to add: 'If you don't like the spelling of the name, have you considered – I don't know – *choosing another name?*'

Like Apple. Pronounced Apple.

Regardless of what you choose to call your child or how you spell it, I think we can all officially agree that it's time for the term 'yummy mummy' to curl up and die. Off to the graveyard of tired pop-culture clichés. The Metrosexual will be there waiting with open arms . . .

'Yummy mummy' is not a term beloved by most mothers. Our general feeling is this: raising children is challenging enough without the expectation you must look hot while you're doing it. What? So you don't resemble a supermodel when you drop the kids at soccer? Shame on you. Pull your socks up, get a blow dry, some botox, $2000 worth of casual cashmere separates and some tight jeans immediately.

What the word 'supermum' was to the eighties (bleurgh), 'yummy mummy' was to the nineties. But we seriously need some new buzzwords. One that's been kicking around for a while but not in the mainstream arena (you'll understand why in a sec) is 'MILF'. I guess you could call the MILF the yummy mummy's raunchy sister, MILF being an acronym for 'Mother I'd Like To . . . know in the biblical sense'.

Sexual attractiveness to young guys is the key feature of the MILF, who is often the inappropriate lust-object of her child's friends. The acronym may be new but MILFs are not. My mother was a MILF. When she'd drop my older brother at high school, he'd get admiring looks from other boys, impressed not only by his hot older 'girlfriend' but that she had, like, a car.

Of course if it's *your* mother who's the MILF, it's not impressive, it's mortifying. My brother was certainly less than thrilled by the comments. It's hard enough to deal with the evidence that your parents actually had sex (i.e. your existence). But having to deal with your friends thinking unnatural thoughts about your mother? Your *MOTH-ER*? That's just too many shades of wrong.

I know one MILF whose fourteen-year-old daughter insists on being dropped two blocks from all school, sport and social activities so as not to have to deal with the leery comments from her male classmates.

Scratch the surface of your childhood memories and you may recall a MILF. 'I went to school with a guy whose mum was the town hairdresser,' remembers one friend. 'She was the classic hot '80s MILF with stonewashed spray-on jeans, blonde perm, hot coral lipstick. Real pretty. After hanging out at his place after school, his friends used to tell him they were going home and then camp on his roof to watch through the skylight as she got nude for her evening bath.'

'We had a MILF at my school,' recalls another friend who went to a Jewish high school. 'She had two stunning daughters who were younger than me, and she'd always come and volunteer at the tuckshop. Boy, oh boy, did the guys line up to buy their kosher pickles from her!'

Ah, the tuckshop. It wasn't just the birthplace of tuck-shop arms, it was also the place where many an adolescent male crush was born and many a MILF did a brisk trade in finger buns and chocolate milk. 'My mum was a mega-MILF,' admitted a friend with the surname McDonald. 'Whenever she did tuckshop duty at my brothers' school, all the boys would line up to be served by her. They called it the Mrs Mac Snack. The line to be served by Mum was always really long and Mum would get embarrassed and feel bad for the non-MILF mums getting no love.'

But what happens when schoolboys grow up? 'A few years ago, my brother had a party at our place,' cringes one friend whose mother was a MILF. 'One of his best mates got *smaaashed* and fully cracked onto my mum. She would have been pushing fifty at the time. This guy was young and cute and, ooh, about, twenty-five. Eeeuw. Mum was a bit flattered and a bit horrified. She'd known him since he was six. He never did come over to our place again . . .'

My favourite story is this one, told to me by a single 27-year-old colleague. 'Last month I bumped into this guy who'd lived next door to me when I was ten. He was about seven years older than me and I'd had a big crush on him. Anyway, he seemed so happy to see me again and I thought it was sweet how he kept asking about my family. He bought me a drink and I told him how Mum and Dad got divorced years ago and caught up on his life. Just before I left, he gave me his card. I was stoked! Until he said, 'Please can you pass on my card to your mother. She was such a beautiful woman; I'd love to see her again.'

I Used to be
Cool Too

I remember when I used to be cool. Vaguely. I think it was in the nineties. I can't recall exactly when I stopped being cool and turned into That Person. Becoming That Person was never part of my plan. In fact it was inconceivable. I was going to be cool forever. A cool adult. A cool parent. A cool boss.

That Person was plainly the antithesis of cool. A dag. A wowser. A prude. That Person was an embarrassment to their children and to themselves. That Person was a fuddy-duddy. That Person said things like 'Back in my day . . .' and 'Kids these days . . .' and ruffled the hair of small children and marvelled 'My goodness, haven't you grown up! I remember when you were *this tall*!' And now I am That Person and I have no idea how it happened.

Sure, I've had inklings over the years that I was losing my edge. Like when listening to triple j went from being automatic to being an effort and then to being an occasional anthropological exercise (what music do hip young people listen to these days?). And when rain went from being a social inconvenience to being 'good for the garden'. And when I began asking sales assistants at Supré to turn down the music 'so I can take my fingers out of my ears for long enough to try on some damn clothes' before becoming aware that my fellow shoppers were wearing school uniforms.

Another clue that you are becoming That Person is when you can't believe how young police are these days.

And when you start saying 'these days'.

But I still wasn't ready to accept my fogey fate. After all, I edited a raunchy women's magazine, you know. I wrote sealed sections about oral sex. I pushed boundaries and envelopes and sometimes also my luck. Once I managed to get my magazine banned in supermarkets and they interviewed me on triple j. I had cred, man.

And then I didn't. I had pop-culture whiplash instead. Because when the moment of clarity arrived, it was jarring. You see, a few weeks ago, I took my son bowling. Nothing wrong with that. Bowling is cool. Cool people bowl now.

Even the shoes have improved. In fact to make bowling even cooler, many venues now resemble nightclubs (well, how nightclubs used to look back when I went to them, back when they played music instead of, ahem, noise).

The lighting is low, the music loud. The place we went to even had giant video screens above the pins at the end of every alley. Modern! Funky!

. . . And yet entirely inappropriate! And if I were prone to hyperbole, which I totally am, I would also add: pornographic smut! That would be the music videos playing on the screens. It was the usual stuff: slutty, near-naked, thrusting, panting women and misogynist black rappers singing about sex and bitches and hos. Music-video shows are banned at my house for this exact reason. I don't expect them while surrounded by bowling kiddies, okay?

As I tried to divert my son's attention towards the game and away from the smut, I looked around at the dozens of small boys and girls hurling their bowling balls towards giant jangling fake breasts and writhing G-string-clad buttocks. My outrage grew with every new clip and I decided to complain to the manager at the end of the game.

In the end, I chickened out. My reasons were utterly self-serving: I wasn't ready to see the image of myself as

That Person reflected in the faces of the twenty-something dudes at the counter. Dudes who would no doubt roll their eyes condescendingly behind my back, if not directly to my front. 'Yeah, yeah, Crazy Old Prude Lady. Like, whatever.' It was enough of a shock to realise that I was That Person. I needed time to digest this revelation in private.

You don't need kids to become That Person. No siree, Bob. As one 33-year-old single girlfriend notes, 'It starts around the same time you begin choosing drinking venues that have soft lighting, soft music and soft chairs.' This same friend recently went to a pub and had a That Person moment. 'I was shocked by what the girls were wearing and how much alcohol they were knocking back. I actually said to my friends, "I used to be cool – what happened? I mean, I used to go out three times a week, dance on tables, leave clubs at 8 a.m., drink too much and wear too little. But we were never as sexually overt as girls are now. We used to dance around our handbags not swing around poles and pash each other." Kids these days . . .'

There are other signs too. Like when you get into the car with your twenty-something colleague who turns on the radio and says, 'God, JT rocks!' and you have no idea what JT means so you just say, 'Oh yeah. Totally rocks. Love JT.' But then you hammer the nail into your fogey coffin by blurting out, 'Look, it's news time. Can I put on the ABC?'

Or when you're invited to house-warming drinks at your neighbour's house but have to leave after one beer 'because *The 7.30 Report* is about to start'. Or when someone suggests dinner in the city and your first question is 'But where will we park?'

Another girlfriend recalls recently going to a nightclub for the first time in years. 'I was so concerned by the state of the girls in there that I was actually walking around asking everyone if they needed water.'

So when exactly did I get older?

After much consideration, I've concluded that I misplaced my ingenue credentials somewhere between getting my bellybutton pierced and ruling out any movie that starts after 6.30 p.m. because I will fall asleep. That narrows it down.

I thought there was merely a blink between those two things but it seems years have passed. And lately, there have been a few key moments when the realisation that I'm no longer a kid has startled me stupid.

Perhaps some will sound familiar to you.

Like working out you've been out of school longer than you were in it. Or being gob-smacked to consider there are people driving cars and having sex who were born in the nineties. *The nineties.*

Or taking your child to an appointment with a doctor who is younger than you. How did that happen? When did doctors and newsreaders and even politicians get so young? Was I napping? Because they used to be old people and suddenly they're not.

It's funny though, how your definition of old changes as you get, well, older. I've been to a handful of 40th birthday parties lately, and sometimes it's a shock to look around the room and see so many bald heads. Nothing wrong with bald but it doesn't exactly shout twenty-two, does it?

Back in 1982 when Prince sang 'Tonight we're going to party like it's 1999', I remember doing some basic arithmetic. Even though 1999 seemed inconceivably far into the future, I deduced that I'd be twenty-nine years old on that particular New Year's Eve. Emphasis on the old. 'Oh, what's the point of a party,' I thought at the time. 'By 1999 I'll be a sad old loser who won't be remotely interested in any type of fun. At midnight I'll probably be home asleep after drinking a cup of herbal tea.'

Oh, wait, I just described my New Year's Eve 2008. Turns out I was off by less than a decade.

I also seem to have reached the age where your children laugh at you when you try to use certain words. Young words. For shizzle. When I said that to my son a few weeks ago, his eyes nearly rolled out of his head. 'Mum, it's really pathetic when old people try to talk young.' He's right about that although I couldn't help protesting, 'Look, I used to be cool, you know! I did!' Pathetic is right.

Still, I did feel a little bit hip when I retold the story to two girlfriends who looked at me blankly. 'Um, what does "for shizzle" mean?' one finally asked. 'Oh, phew,' said the other. 'I thought it was just me. I have no idea either. Never heard of it.'

It was a struggle to keep the cool smugness out of my voice as I explained that it derived from Snoop Doggy Dog and was slang for 'for sure'. In truth, I'm not actually certain of this, but whatever.

I know you're only as old as you feel (or, as sleazy men like to guffaw, 'You're only as old as the woman you feel') but sometimes the disconnect between your actual age and your internal one can be jarring.

A girlfriend was jarred in such a way earlier this year

when she attended her nephew's high-school footy game. 'I was walking through the crowd and found myself inadvertently checking out a few of the older boys and thinking, "Oh, you're a bit hot" and then realising that I'm twenty years older then them and possibly technically a criminal for even having such thoughts. In my head, I was a high-school girl again but they were probably going, "Sad nanna." '

Then there are times when the generation gap leaps out of nowhere to smack you over the head. Like a few months ago when I was invited by a record-company mate to see a showcase by a new band.

I took a girlfriend with me, and as we waited at the bar for our wine, I launched into a loud and detailed moan about how the baby wasn't sleeping through the night because he was teething. Is that not what people in nightclubs discuss?

Anyway, the showcase was great and afterwards I met two of the girls in the band who were about twenty. 'I don't go to clubs much any more,' I told them, making conversation, 'so I was quite chuffed that I'd pulled together a suitable look until I got into the car and discovered I had Fuzzy Felt in my hair.'

They both looked at me blankly.

'You know, Fuzzy Felt!' I repeated. Blankety blank. That's when I remembered they were twenty and had no clue what I was talking about. Try to explain what a Fuzzy Felt is. Go on. Try. It's challenging, even when you're not in a noisy nightclub. For shizzle.

Another indication of my age is that I've never kissed a girl. I feel faintly disappointed about this because, as a married mother of three, it seems my opportunity to tick that pop-culture experience off my list has probably faded. Now that I don't hang out in nightclubs or go to parties or take drugs or stay up all night drinking, there's not much chance of it happening in that casual, spontaneous way younger women tend to do it.

There's not much girl–girl action at your local playground or weekend barbecue, I find.

However, in certain younger circles, sexuality has gone open slather and heterosexuals are suddenly like, so . . . straight. Square. Nerdy.

The cool kids are all hetroflexible, polysexual, ambisexual, pansensual, bi-curious, bi-queer, metroflexible, hetero-sexual with lesbian tendencies – or just sexual. Celebrities (only female ones, mind you) are falling over themselves to announce their bisexuality or drop their same-sex experimentation into interviews or photo opportunities.

It's all about keeping your sexual options open, people. You never know who you might want to grope tomorrow.

In one New York co-ed high school I read about, there's an informal daily gathering called the Cuddle Puddle, where boys and girls meet between classes to loll about on the floor draped all over each other while kissing and cuddling. Boys and boys, girls and boys, girls and girl . . . there are no pigeon-holes here. These teenagers don't feel they have to define their sexuality let alone that their sexuality has to define them. Times have changed and, for some, it's no longer about being gay or straight or lesbian. It's just about being.

In the article I read, seventeen-year-old Cuddle Puddler Elle used herself as a window into this new sexual dynamic, describing to *New York* magazine how she met her boyfriend at a recent party: 'I kissed five people and, like, hooked up with two going beyond kissing. One of them was a boy and one of them was a girl. The reason I started hooking up with the guy is because he was making out with this other guy and he came back and was like, "I have to prove that I'm straight." And I was standing right there and that's how our relationship started.' Wow. That's, like, so romantic.

When I was at high school, few things would have been more socially ostracising than rumours of same-sex tendencies, let alone actual gay pashing in public. But happily, many of today's teens are a whole lot more accepting of sexual diversity, both in others and in themselves. And why wouldn't they be?

If you're under twenty-five, there's actually very little shock value left in kissing someone with matching genitalia. If anything, it's been replaced with cynicism. 'I think genuine bi guys are the rarest of all sexual incantations,' scoffs a twenty-something guy I know. 'The overwhelming majority of bi girls are phony straight girls looking to make themselves seem cool or sexy.'

Yes, there is still some resistance. Not everyone younger than you is jumping into the Cuddle Puddle with gay abandon.

One of my female Gen Y friends makes this observation: 'I think it's very much still a case of bi girls being hot, whereas bi guys are still viewed as potential disease vessels. And despite trying to be outwardly open-minded by saying it wouldn't bother them, I don't think any of my female friends would be cool with their dude swapping holes for poles.'

A male Gen Yer agrees: 'I have one guy friend who is genuinely bi. He is one of the most confident, outgoing guys

I've ever met and his philosophy is simply if he meets someone and he's attracted to them as a person, it doesn't matter
if they're male or female. I've often liked to think I would be
the same – but I've never been attracted to a guy. If any of
my girlfriends had been born the same person but a man,
would I have been attracted to them? Uh, no, they would
just be the first person I call to see if they wanna go have a
beer or buy some sneakers.'

When I asked a couple of my girlfriends who have
pashed girls why they think I never have, they said it's
because I'm too straight. In a lifestyle sense. It seems if
you're over twenty-five and fundamentally heterosexual, you
need something else to help push your boundaries. As one
thirty-something puts it: 'When you add drugs or alcohol
and the possibility of a threesome; suddenly no one is "bi" or
"gay"; everyone's just wild.'

I get it. Labels are so over. Kissing a girl no longer even
counts as experimenting. It's just an experience. Like riding a camel. Or bungy jumping. Or climbing the Harbour
Bridge. Or getting a tattoo. No wait, that's not at all like
kissing a girl or riding a camel. The consequences of a tattoo
are somewhat longer lasting.

***

I'm reminded of this every time I go to the beach where I'm often surprised to notice how many girls have tattoos. Wait, I shouldn't say girls because I mean women. In their twenties, thirties and forties. Pregnant women. Women with toddlers and mortgages. Women with primary-school kids and sensible haircuts. Women who drive station wagons. Women who go to Michael Bublé concerts. They're all inked.

Like me, you might never have realised this because many of them have tattoos in discreet places, only visible in the shower, at the beach or during sex.

And the women who are tattooed in more public areas often cover them in formal situations, like my friend Kerri who has a few tatts including one on the back of her shoulder.

'I have a love–hate relationship with that one,' she says. 'When I'm in me-mode, out with friends or just my family, I love it. But I do feel self-conscious about it at school functions or when meeting a teacher. I worry about being labelled as the "tattooed mother". Most of the time I just deal with the awkwardness, but at school, I cover it up with a top.'

My beach observations were confirmed when I recently read an article declaring that after a popularity lull in the '80s and '90s, tattoos have become huge again. Literally. Women are apparently rejecting discreet little symbols, roses, love hearts and dolphins for bigger, bolder designs.

'Girls want tattoos that flow with the contours of their bodies,' tattoo artist 'Moldi' was reported as saying. 'The scrag tag has really died off.' (FYI: a 'scrag tag', also know as a 'tramp stamp', is apparently a tattoo on your lower back. I never knew it was called this. Presumably, neither did all the women you see at the beach who have them.)

The move from small to large tattoos for women is wonderful news for the parents of teenage girls who may still be under the deluded impression that they can prevent their daughters from permanently marking themselves. Newsflash: forgeddaboudit.

My uncle discovered this the hard way when my eighteen-year-old cousin returned from a gap-year trip overseas with a tattoo of her best friend's name written in Sanskrit all the way up the side of her torso. I think it looks quite beautiful. Her father does not share my view. Meanwhile, my cousin insists she has 'no regrets'. This is not surprising given she only had it done four months ago.

My own tattoo is in a discreet area and rarely seen by strangers. Except this one time at the Logies when I spontaneously decided to show it to a number of people on the dance floor at 2 a.m. They were admittedly gay, but still, I'd rather not discuss it in this book or, in fact, ever again.

Where was I?

Right. Tattoos.

So why do grown women do it? Often, it's as a way to reclaim something of yourself or, possibly, an early life crisis. The last grasp at cool.

As one friend explains: 'I got mine after my first two kids were born. I'd always loved tatts but just didn't have the confidence [read 'need to rebel'] until my mid-thirties.' What do her kids think? Not much, as it turns out. 'Sometimes my eight-year-old touches the one on my shoulder but they mostly ignore it. They've never even asked if it hurt or why I got it. I definitely did it as a small act of rebellion, and it annoys me that nearly every young girl has one now, because it means I'm not so special.'

Or rebellious.

Bikies are really going to have to find a new way to look tough. When mothers' groups and school canteens are hotbeds of ink? When tattoo parlours practically require a crèche? Dude, your street cred is getting seriously compromised.

Indeedy, it seems we're on the cusp of a fascinating

generational shift. If tattoos have traditionally been about rebellion, how will the kids of all these tattooed mothers rebel?

Maybe by doing Meals on Wheels. Or getting married and staying that way.

The reverse psychology approach is one I've adopted with my own children for years. To them, tattoos are as unremarkable as pierced ears. So many of the women in their life have them. Aunties, godmothers, babysitters, family friends, it's practically a by-product of being female. Like boobs.

Whenever we see a tattoo parlour, I always exclaim, 'Come on! I think it's time you got a real tattoo. It won't be too bad. It's just like 200 needles going into you all at once. You'll be fine!' This always elicits the desired shriek of horror and I silently pat myself on the back for being a brilliant and crafty parent.

Until they come home one day with tattoos all over their faces, at which point I will acknowledge that my strategy may have been slightly flawed.

Memo to self: adopt same approach to piercing.

When I was a kid, getting your ears pierced was something girls negotiated with their parents when they were around fourteen years old. Some girls weren't even allowed to pierce their ears until they left school. (One of my friends still isn't allowed and she just turned thirty-four.)

Those innocent times are as dated as Boy George posters. These days, bemused mums and horrified dads are being begged, bribed and bullied into allowing their daughters to get all sorts of things pierced. Things like bellybuttons. Noses. Eyebrows. Tongues.

I know two sets of parents who recently caved – one to a bellybutton, the other to a nose piercing. In the space of a couple of months, both mothers phoned to ask my advice on how to handle their daughters' pleas for piercings. Having known both girls since they were toddlers, I surprised myself by spluttering nanna things like 'totally inappropriate' and 'in my day . . .'. Then I hung up the phone and cringed a little bit, partly at the thought of these beautiful girls sticking holes in themselves and partly at my own hypocrisy.

I got my bellybutton pierced when I was about twenty-one (note: twenty-one not fourteen). A colleague and I were bored at work one day and spontaneously decided to have something pierced in our lunch hour. This was way before celebrities had made bellybutton rings as common as lip gloss; back when piercings were edgy! Exciting! Fashion-forward!

Well, they're the words I muttered to myself like a mantra as I lay on the table in The Piercing Urge, having my stomach examined by a Goth girl with rings through both eyebrows, her bottom lip and the bridge of her nose. And they were just the visible ones. The laminated folder of piercings in the waiting room was very enlightening and utterly nauseating. Who knew that scrotums could do that? Or that any scrotum-owner would want to?

Back on the table, I learnt that not all bellybuttons are suitable for piercing – outies need not apply. Fortunately, my innie was declared 'wicked cool' by Ms Goth, who then handed me a form waiving my right to sue if any part of my body, like, fell off or something after it was pierced. Of course I signed with barely a glimpse because by now I was too embarrassed to chicken out – even when I learnt that Goth-girl wasn't going to use a piercing gun (like they do for ears), but a thick needle. Like a knitting needle. Since I really love needles of all kinds, this was a particularly exciting development. Oh, happy day.

The pain was bad and weird. Since my brain had never known bellybutton pain before, it registered extreme surprise along with agony. However, like childbirth, the pain memory faded fast and I was left with a new hole in my body and an instruction leaflet on how to care for it. My friend wasn't so lucky.

Being in her early thirties, she reasoned that her midriff years were behind her, so instead of her bellybutton, she'd elected to pierce the top part of her ear. A bit punk. A bit rock 'n' roll. What she didn't know was that ear cartilage is one of the most high-risk piercing sites. Evil infections are common. Within days, that's what happened and her doctor prescribed antibiotics.

Then the infection got suddenly worse. Her ear and one side of her head swelled up (are you listening, teenage girls?) and her doctor then prescribed the emergency room. Stat. She ended up in hospital for two weeks with a potentially life-threatening golden staph infection, hooked up to intravenous antibiotics that were the only thing that could kill the super bug.

Is there a moral to this story? I guess it would be this: 'Beware of becoming a fashion victim.'

My bellybutton ring didn't last long. A couple of months. There were two reasons for this. Firstly, it never healed properly. They don't tell you this in the brochure. But the constant rubbing of clothes and catching on jeans meant it was always irritated and perennially crusty. I'm sorry I just used the word crusty but there really is no other that will suffice and I think it's an important balance to the other words more often used by those considering a piercing, like 'cool' and 'sexy'. Best you add 'crusty' to your list of adjectives, okay?

The second reason I removed it is because I started dating a boy who hated it and thought it was disgusting (*see* crusty). I still have the scar.

I've never regretted my tattoo, however. Not for a moment. This is probably because I waited until my 30th birthday to get one so I could be certain it wasn't the impulsive action of a 22-year-old (*see* piercing). Despite the warnings from some people who insisted it would be an appalling embarrassment when I was an old lady, I've always believed the opposite. I think that will be the best part, that unexpected contrast between grey hair and a tatt. I look forward to that.

In the meantime, I've decided I need to dance more. This epiphany came to me suddenly one evening at a work function where one of my favourite artists was performing a few songs. I rarely see any live music because I get too sleepy too early to go to gigs. Rock on!

Anyhow, on this particular (early) night, I made my way

to the front of the small, muted crowd, the front still being a good 10 metres away from the stage. Instantly, into the empty space in front of us launched two women. Sober women. Women unlike the rest of the audience, who were standing around clutching drinks and tapping feet discreetly, their veneer of cool intact. These two? Whooping it up. Moving to the music and singing the words. Major whoop.

While I listened to the music, I watched the two women dancing with an emotion I couldn't place for a moment. Oh, wait, I know. It's envy. Then, since I'm incapable of having a private thought, I leaned over to one of my workmates and shouted into his ear, 'I really wish I didn't care what anyone thought of me so I could be free and dance like that.' He nodded. 'Me too.'

So why couldn't I? Why was I so inhibited? Here's why: dancing in public is intimidating and exposing. I'm not a bad dancer. In fact, I'll go out on a limb and say I'm quite good, dammit. I have rhythm and some funky moves. But I never get a chance to cut loose because of my innate fear of looking like a goose.

The ridiculous part is, of course, that no one is looking at me. No one could give a toss whether I'm dancing. When I went to a Robbie Williams concert a few years ago, did the audience turn, as one, to look at me bouncing awkwardly in front of my seat? They did not. Were they all too busy grooving to Robbie or obsessing that everyone was looking at *them*? They were.

With me at this concert happened to be a girlfriend who has no insecure dancing hang-ups. As expected, she was the first person in our section to leap to her feet, a good two or three songs before the rest of us shrugged off our self-consciousness and awkwardly joined her.

So who got the best value out of their ticket – her or me? Who gets the best value out of their *life*? Afterwards, over caprioskas, we talked about dancing. 'Yeah, I'm always the first person on the dance floor,' she confirmed, glancing over my shoulder to asses the space in front of the bar. 'Dancing is my number one way to de-stress, relax, have fun, feel confident – every feel-good endorphin within me is released. I actually get pissed off if I don't have a dance on weekends.'

I hear you, sister. I remember that feeling from a lifetime ago. Until I grew up and became inhibited. Surprisingly, this friend insists she too is an inhibited person. 'The other five days of the week, I'm utterly hung-up about what people think of me – at work and in my social life. I worry because I didn't go to a fancy school, because I don't earn as much money, because I don't have an amazing wardrobe. But on the dance floor, I can leave all that behind.'

This friend also maintains she doesn't need a glass of confidence to dance. But many other dancing queens do. 'After a few drinks I'll be first on the floor and won't stop dancing for hours,' admits another friend who's in her late twenties and goes out a lot. 'But before that initial drop of alcohol, I'm paralysed. It's born of insecurity, I guess, a fear of being judged.'

If many women have a fear of looking like a knob, most men have this same fear squared. I can't say I know any men of any age or sexual persuasion who aspire to be John Travolta or any of the *Solid Gold* dancers.

On dance floors, men don't tend to put their beers on the ground and dance in a small circle around them. Which is a shame really, if you ask me.

Italy is an exception to the general rule of dancing inhibitions. In Italian nightclubs, many men dance enthusiastically while watching themselves in the mirror. Literally. In. Front. Of. The. Mirror. Just them and the mirror. Really. And they're not even drunk when they do it. Just vain and confident in equal measure.

But gender aside, my burning question is where? *Where!*

Where do you dance when you're an adult? A nightclub? A moshpit? A table? The older you get, the more married you are, the more children you have, the fewer your opportunities to dance. Outside of a wedding or a Wiggles concert.

My ideal venue would be somewhere that plays music with words and a tune. Not just a synthetic techno beat that hurts your ears. No smoke. Open early. Snacks. My lounge room is looking excellent.

There was no dancing at my twenty-year school reunion. More's the pity.

I've decided that school reunions are what you get when you cross a job interview with speed dating. Fast, slightly awkward, intimidating and exciting all at once. With lots of questions.

Things kicked off predictably when I forgot to RSVP, despite receiving a printed invitation and several email reminders. Hello, recalcitrant teenager, I remember you well. Having been so slack, I was one of half a dozen naughty girls whose names were circulated on a group email from the school (where the reunion was being held) asking us to *please* confirm our attendance. This was enough to instantly ignite dormant banter in a flurry of 'reply-all' emails resplendent with forgotten nicknames and highly spirited piss-taking.

Suddenly, unexpectedly and delightfully, we were fifteen again, except with laugh lines instead of pimples and taxes instead of pocket money.

School friends are unlike any other people in your life. They fly straight under your adult radar, directly to your inner child. No matter who you think you are or who you're trying to be, your schoolmates know your DNA. Even if you think you left it behind with your Clearasil and your lunchbox.

Twenty years later, I was fascinated to know how everyone's lives had turned out. Like skipping to the end of a book you put down and forgot about. However, not everyone shared my excitement. A third of our year didn't come, and while geography was responsible for some of the no-shows, others perhaps had more complex reasons for staying away.

Like birthdays and Christmas, reunions force you to do a mental stocktake of your life – compared to those around you and compared to your own expectations. This can be confronting. I understand that. There have been several periods since leaving school when I would have done anything to avoid the 'So, what are you doing now?' question, even if it was asked with benevolence not judgement.

On the night, I quickly learnt to keep my opening question broad and non-threatening. Not 'What do you do?' or 'How many kids do you have?'. The measures of a life are diverse and unique and not always easy to encapsulate in a sound bite.

As the wine flowed, someone grabbed the microphone to thank the organisers, and soon everyone was jumping up to share memories. The mood quickly turned rebellious, with a group of girls congregating defiantly outside the principal's office to smoke. Most weren't even smokers but couldn't resist the opportunity to be rebels without fear of suspension.

Just as things were becoming a little derailed, one girl took to the microphone to share her feelings about being reunited with people she hadn't seen for decades. Having lived in Korea for a while, she said there was a Korean word, *cheong*, which is the effect of spending a lot of time or living through an experience with others. 'It means, even if you're not on exactly the same wavelength with these people,' she explained, 'you're connected forever because you've travelled through part of your life together. And what's more, you take a keen interest in them and genuinely wish them well.'

She brought the house down. With all our half-drunk,

excitable nattering, none of us had been able to articulate how surprisingly connected we still felt after all these years.

And then it was time to adjourn to the pub, the same one we'd tried to sneak into every weekend as teens.

I'm going to admit right now that a small, deluded part of my brain expected to be asked for ID at the door. The Pavlovian response is a strong one because those familiar butterflies instantly appeared in my stomach as we approached the entrance. And when we sailed through, I experienced that little rush of euphoria as though I'd got away with something.

Once upstairs in the bar, we peered around in the semi-darkness for somewhere to sit. Evidently, in bar terms, we were not match fit. Like short-sighted sheep, we stumbled towards a quiet area and plonked ourselves down on the couches.

Almost immediately, someone told us to move. 'Sorry, this area is reserved for a private function,' said the staff member. 'Maybe it's reserved for us,' ventured someone hopefully. 'No, it's a young person's party,' came the reply.

Oh, listen. It's the sound of several dozen 37-year-old women cringing simultaneously. As one, we all stood and made our way huffily to the exit. 'Right,' said someone, possibly me, 'we'll just take our *old lady money* and go spend it elsewhere.'

Faster than you could say *cheong*, we were merrily treading a well-worn path to the other local pub, in the same way we used to spend every Friday night traipsing between the two, depending on which bouncer took the most flexible approach to allowing underage girls onto a licensed premises. Just like old times, except instead of sneaking into my house quietly so as not to wake my sleeping parents (and alert them to the fact I broke curfew), I tiptoed in to kiss my sleeping kids.

Had we stayed in the bar with the 'young people', we could have played this new party game I recently devised over dinner with Gen Y friends.

It's called Feel Your Age, and to play it, you need to find several people under twenty-six and at least one person of your own vintage. Then, start reminiscing about the '70s and '80s and watch the youngsters go blank and look puzzled. It's fun. Especially in the bonus round when you challenge them to a quick quiz called What Am I Talking About?

Here's a sample:

Me: 'Do the right thing.'

Gen Y1: 'A movie by Spike Jones.'

Gen Y2: 'Um, something your parents would say?'

Correct answer: An ad campaign urging us not to litter at a time when people routinely threw rubbish out of cars or dropped it in the street. Chorus sung by kiddy choir.

Me: 'Air Supply.'

Gen Y1: 'One of those "crash investigation" programs.'

Gen Y2: 'Yeah! Was it, like, a hospital show?'

Correct answer: Australian soft-rock group that sang sloppy ballads. Hits included 'Lost In Love', 'The One That You Love', 'All Out Of Love'.

Me: 'D-D-D-Decoré.'

Gen Y1: 'Something to do with someone who had a stutter?'

Gen Y2: 'A nightclub.'

Correct answer: A shampoo campaign featuring people singing in the shower into shampoo bottles.

Me: 'Hall & Oates.'

Gen Y1: 'Um . . . muesli?'

Gen Y2: 'Was it that cat and dog movie? Oh, hang on, that was Milo and Otis.'

Correct answer: Another '80s band comprising a tall white dude and a short dark dude. Hits included 'Man Eater'.

Me: 'Joyce Mayne.'

Gen Y1: 'A fashion label.'

Gen Y2: 'A feminist.'

Correct answer: Strange old lady with screechy Cockney accent and coloured hair who appeared in ads for a furniture chain of the same name.

Me: 'Life be in it.'

Gen Y1: 'Was it a lifestyle program?'

Gen Y2: 'A website!'

Correct answer: Animated ad campaign urging Australians to be less fat and more active. It starred fat couch-potato Norm and his aerobics-loving Lycra-clad wife whose main goal was getting Norm's fat ass off the lounge.

Me: 'Zooper Doopers.'

Gen Y1: 'A type of party drug.'

Gen Y2: 'A boy band.'

Correct answer: Tube-shaped ice-block. Fifteen cents at the canteen.

Me: 'Romper Room.'

Gen Y1: 'A nightclub.'

Gen Y2: 'An all-in-one outfit. No, wait, that's a romper suit.'

Correct answer: A kids' show hosted by Miss Helena. Especially exciting if she said she could 'see you' through her magic mirror at the end of the show and called your name.

Me: 'Chuck a lucky seven.'

Gen Y1: 'Ah . . . something someone with a gambling addiction says too often?'

Gen Y2: 'A cricket thing.'

Correct answer: Catchy ad campaign for Channel Seven in the '80s where people 'chucked' a lucky seven by holding up five fingers and then two – with palm facing forward so as not to be rude.

Me: 'You're soaking in it!'

Gen Y1: 'Um . . .'

Gen Y2: 'Being in the shit – not dissimilar to "You made your bed, lie in it"?'

Correct answer: Catchphrase for ad campaign for Palmolive detergent where 'Marge' did some kind of market-research test where she surprised people by soaking their hands in dishwashing liquid. Unsure of the official relevance of Marge but vaguely remember her wearing a uniform of some kind like a nurse.

Me: 'The Grim Reaper goes to a bowling alley.'
Gen Y1: 'Is this the start of a famous joke?'
Gen Y2: 'Was there also a rabbi and a priest or something?'
Correct answer: Famous AIDS awareness campaign in the '80s conceived by Siimon Reynolds. Showed all different types of people as pins in a bowling alley, all victim to the bowling ball (representing AIDS) launched by the Grim Reaper. Still able to provoke shudder of fear in Gen Xers even today.

Me: '*Solid Gold* dancers.'
Gen Y1: 'Cheerleaders?'
Gen Y2: 'A type of acid trip.'
Correct answer: The dancers on the *Solid Gold* show, hosted by Dionne Warwick in the '70s. Famous for their elaborate formations at the end of each dance and glamorous costumes, much like Madonna's latest look.

In conclusion, the '70s and '80s were a very bossy time, weren't they? We were urged to get fit, stop littering, wear sunscreen, chuck a lucky seven, wear condoms, wear seatbelts, stop drinking and driving . . . it was exhausting.

Something I find equally exhausting today is the way the media is so generation-obsessed, painstakingly defining the characteristics of Ys, Xs and Baby Boomers.

Well, dividing humanity into homogenised Happy-Meal boxes may have its purpose, but there will always be a bunch of people who don't conform to their assigned letter of the alphabet. Sound like you? Maybe you're a GRUP.

GRUPS are 35-plus-year-old men and women who look, talk, act and dress like people who are twenty-two years old. An XY hybrid. A social group that is technically of one generation (X) but behaves like another (Y).

The inelegant name, GRUP, was invented by writer Adam Sternbergh, who identified this sub-genre in an American magazine article. He explains it as 'a nerdy reference to an old *Star Trek* episode in which Kirk and crew land on a planet run entirely by kids, who call grown-ups "grups". All the adults have been killed off by a terrible virus, which also slows the natural ageing process, so the kids are trapped in a state of extended prepubescence. They will never grow up. And they are running the show.'

Look around or possibly in the mirror and you'll have an a-ha moment as you recognise GRUPS everywhere. As Sternbergh explains, 'They are a generation or two of affluent, urban adults who are now happily sailing through their thirties and forties, and even *fifties*, clad in beat-up sneakers and cashmere hoodies, content that they can enjoy all the good parts of being a grown-up with none of the bad parts.'

The good parts include grown-up pay cheques, somewhere nice to live and the pleasures of family. The bad parts would be management seminars, sensible haircuts and classic-hits radio stations.

Remember being twenty-two and all the cool things you wanted but couldn't afford? GRUPS not only know what's cool, they also have the cash to buy it and the confidence to carry it off. And this convergence of cash, cool and confidence makes them easily identifiable. Not to mention a very sexy marketing target.

GRUPS wear $400 jeans designed to look old the first time they're worn. They carry expensive Diesel messenger bags instead of briefcases. They have expensive bed-head haircuts and expensive distressed T-shirts. They own multiple pairs of sneakers. They often have tattoos. They go snowboarding.

GRUPS might wear Converse High Tops while pushing $900 prams around the park. They might grow a beard in an ironic way.

To better understand and identify GRUPS, it's also worth noting what GRUPS are not.

This is not a generational mutton-dressed-as-lamb situation. GRUPS are not try-hards. They are not desperate or sad or tragic or wishing to be younger.

GRUPS simply don't comply with the conventional adult wisdom that says growing up means you have to, like, grow up. For GRUPS, getting older doesn't mean having to get a Hillary Clinton haircut or a pair of boat shoes. It doesn't mean having to shave every day or tossing out your distressed denim. Nor does it mean giving up moshing just because your lower back hurts sometimes – hey, unlike the young moshers, GRUPS can claim their osteopath bills on their expensive private health insurance!

GRUPS are not Adultescents. Remember them? They were the Peter Pan branch of Gen Xers who didn't want to take on the responsibilities of adulthood and delayed things like commitment, marriage, kids and mortgages. GRUPS aren't like this. GRUPS get married and have kids. GRUPS love kids. They just don't necessarily parent conventionally.

Parent-GRUPS are more likely to bring their kid to a music festival than take them to a Wiggles concert.

GRUPS know that three-year-olds have lousy taste in music and TV shows. That's why they're likely to censor the *Teletubbies*, discourage all things Disney and direct their kids straight to *The Simpsons* and Pixar movies so Mummy and Daddy get to have a subversive laugh at the same time. Failing that, they'll just download *The Muppet Show* from iTunes.

GRUPS close the generation gap between X and Y. They close it because they straddle both generations authentically and without pretence. They close it with music, with fashion, with lifestyle and with their attitudes. They close it with jeans and T-shirts and sneakers and technology.

Quite simply, GRUPS found the age they liked being – early twenties – and decided to stay there. But wait, they're not stuck in their own youth: if you're under twenty-five, they're stuck in *your* youth.

There's another interesting new social hybrid: the New Hedonists. They party hard – really hard – and then do some downward dogs. Instead of doing decadence 24/7 like, say, Kate Moss or Keith Richards, New Hedonists party part-time.

If you had to summarise them in a sentence it would be this: 'Can I please have a line of coke and a wheatgrass shot?'

In actual fact, you can't buy cocaine and wheatgrass in the same place. You do need to go to different places to get your drugs and your health food, but New Hedonists ingest both with equal enthusiasm.

Some do it on weekends, others do it seasonally. While they're living clean, they're scrupulously clean, limiting all toxins and impurities in a smug way that makes you want to smack them a little bit. For their smugness. Then they go headlong in the opposite direction towards excess.

'I go off on the weekend,' admits Amy, a 32-year-old banker who regularly parties until 3 a.m. on Friday and Saturday nights with the help of amphetamines and vodka. 'But during the week I'm really good. I take vitamins, I do Pilates and meditate. I don't even have a glass of wine.'

Bravo, Amy, ten points for hypocrisy. But most New Hedonists see nothing hypocritical in the extremity of their behaviour. It's just how they live. They even manage to be pious about the fact they only eat organic and only drink decaf – when they're not snorting lines of coke off the toilet cistern in a nightclub with a stranger at 2 a.m.

My friend Max is like that and I find it really annoying. Inviting him over to dinner is hell. He doesn't 'do' carbs or dairy, he's vegan and he eschews wheat and sugar. He works out like a demon and goes on yoga retreats twice a year. He's a Buddhist. But every Saturday night he'll knock back scotch like water and obliterate himself by 10 p.m. Then he'll keep drinking until he vomits, falls over or falls over in his own vomit. If I ever dare question his lifestyle or suggest he acquaint himself with moderation at both ends of the spectrum, he gets painfully condescending and manages to accuse me of being both uptight (for not partying like him) and unhealthy (for eating dairy and – gasp – wheat).

At those glamorous health retreats where people go to detox and do tai chi at sunrise, the biggest spikes in guests apparently occur in the first week in January and the week after Mardi Gras.

This is typical for the New Hedonists who use healthy living as a form of penance for their sins. 'Most weekends I have an ecstasy or two and stay out until dawn,' explains Belinda, a thirty-year-old real-estate agent. 'Every Monday after work, I do a really hard Bikram yoga class and sweat out all the toxins. I pick up some macrobiotic takeaway on the way home and I'm in bed by 9 p.m. By Tuesday, I've put the memory of the weekend behind me and the rest of the week is really low-key. The most outrageous thing I do is have a decaf soy latte. But then the weekend rolls around again and I feel like I deserve to let loose. Then the whole cycle starts again.'

Ah, the balance sheet approach. This is the way many New Hedonists justify their behaviour: purity cancels out depravity, yoga cancels out cocaine and herbal tea cancels out eleven Bacardi Breezers. It's lifestyle logic of the most twisted variety but not really surprising for a generation who invented the quick fix.

Not that all New Hedonists are necessarily young. Many are in their thirties or forties and may even be parents. These are the ones who use partying as a way to feel like they're still twenty-two. 'I'm so responsible in every way,' says Gemma, who is thirty-seven and married with kids. 'I'm the full soccer mum during the week, but my husband and I like to send the kids to their grandparents every second weekend and go out partying and gambling all night. Just because we're parents doesn't mean we're like, you know, middle-aged and boring.'

Belinda expressed a similar sentiment. 'If I didn't go out clubbing and I just lived my clean weekday life, I'd feel like a nanna. I'm young and single and I want to have fun. I love my tofu but I also love being a bit wild and dancing on tables.'

Myself, I've never been good at juggling two such drastically different lifestyles simultaneously. When I used to party, I'd pity anyone tucked up early in bed for having such dull lives. Now that being tucked up early is my absolute definition of a top night, I can't imagine why anyone would want to go out past 10 p.m. I'm also less extreme, living less on the outer edges of cocaine or yoga. In fact, I do neither.

These days, my biggest vice is probably consumerism, particularly in the form of buying clothes I don't need.

Dear Fitting Rooms Without Mirrors On The Inside: I hate you.

If I could buy a T-shirt with these words on the front, I would. In fact I'm considering hiring one of those little skywriting planes to share this sentiment with the world.

A while ago, it became woefully apparent that I needed some new jeans. In the same way I imagine Warren Buffett or Bill Gates wakes up and feels certain he needs some new money. Got rather a lot already, admittedly, but can you ever have enough? Probably yes, but I've not reached that happy point yet so off I went to buy more jeans.

What other item of clothing can make you feel instantly younger when you get it right and uncomfortably daggy when you suspect you're getting it wrong? What other item of clothing can be worn appropriately by four generations simultaneously – as recently occurred at my grandfather's birthday barbecue?

When you feel that fashion has become a planet far too alien to navigate, there's nothing like a new pair of jeans to recalibrate your wardrobe. Denim is the ultimate wardrobe building block.

Somehow by osmosis, I knew that the current jeans trends were 'boyfriend', 'ripped' and 'pale denim'.

After defiantly sitting out the last major trend due to a way too high degree of difficulty (high-waisted jeans, anyone? *Anyone?*), I've been reluctant to venture into tricky denim. But since bootleg jeans seem determined to remain uncool for the foreseeable future (so the arbiters of such things assure me), its time to update my look. Especially since the only clothes I wear besides jeans are called 'pyjamas'.

This is how I came to be inside a mirror-free fitting room with a pile of denim at my feet, muttering rude words under my breath. Reluctantly and rather huffily propelled into the shop in search of a mirror, I was intercepted – excruciatingly – by a twelve-year-old sales assistant with a facial piercing and a condescending attitude.

The first pair I'd tried were boyfriend jeans – an '80s throwback made popular again by various celebrities. The fit is loose, the crotch is low. As their name suggests, they look like you borrowed jeans from your boyfriend. But why do that for free when you can spend several hundred dollars on boyfriend jeans made especially for women?

As the very young sales girl intruded on my personal and mental space by standing too close and talking too much, I pondered if having a husband meant I was too old for boyfriend jeans? Do they make husband jeans?

'I'm not sure about the size . . .' I muttered out loud, which was a mistake because Miley decided it was a question and proceeded to answer it, in that patronising singsong voice people use with small children and dogs. 'Nooooo! That's the look! It's called the BOYFRIEND-JEAN.' I tried to shoot Miley a withering look, but I was so keen to escape scrutiny in the middle of the shop floor, I decided there was no time to be wasted trying to explain that I knew perfectly well what the jeans were called and why.

Back in my mirrorless cell, I knew I was on a fast track to mutton when I found myself wondering, 'Is my ass too old for these jeans?' as I slipped on a pair of ripped-to-shreds light denim ones. No mirror required for that answer. And, Miley, if you think I'm stepping out into the fluorescent light to have you lie to me and insist I look fanTAStic, you had a big bowl of crazy for breakfast.

An hour later, I stumbled onto the footpath with no dignity and a pair of unremarkable jeans that were the best of an inappropriate bunch, bought in a desperate bid to get away from Miley and make her stop talking to me.

In the sanctuary of my own home – with mirrors and without condescending commentary – I realised immediately that the jeans were a hundred shades of wrong and returned them the next day.

A few weeks later, when my shopping strength had returned and I'd quizzed a few fashion friends about where to go, I tottered off to a cool little store a few suburbs away. There, I was quickly taken under the wing of that rare breed of sales assistant – the one who is so lovely and so clever she makes you want to buy everything in the shop and especially whatever she's wearing. I'm like an imprintable duckling when I find sales-girl chemistry like that. It opens my heart and my wallet like magic.

Informative without being pushy, sweet without being insincere, honest yet persuasive, 22-year-old Xanthe helped me navigate dozens of styles and narrow down my picks to two pairs: a boyfriend style and a slim fit. I also bought the scarf Xanthe was wearing, and if I could have bought her hair (long, dark and tousled), I would have done that too. I may still. Denim mission accomplished. Suck on that, Miley.

Living in the Now

I've cracked it. Finally, I've worked out the difference between men and women and it's this: men are excellent at living in the present moment and women are rubbish at it.

I came to this conclusion after buying a book called *The Power Of Now* by Eckhart Tolle. I found the first few chapters interesting before I added it to my giant collection of Books I Will Never Finish. You see, my new-age concentration span falls off a cliff after about forty-five minutes, so under my bedside table is a graveyard of books on happiness, being a better parent, optimism, Buddhism and assorted other –isms.

I'm hoping to absorb their contents via osmosis while I sleep, which is a pretty optimistic idea so perhaps it's working.

Anyway, I've realised lately how shocking I am at living in the now, hence my interest in buying another book in the hope of fixing myself. My symptoms of future-dwelling include vagueness, anxiety and distractedly banging into furniture. I hadn't directly associated any of these things with an inability to be present until I read page 50 of *The Power Of Now*: '*Unease, anxiety, tension, stress, worry – all forms of fear – are caused by too much future and not enough presence. Guilt, regret, resentment, grievances, sadness, bitterness . . . are caused by too much past, and not enough presence.*'

Sound like anyone you know?

A few days after we brought our first baby home from hospital, my husband and I were blissfully marvelling at the perfection of our son's teeny tiny little fingers. Suddenly, my eyes filled with tears. 'What's wrong?' my husband asked. My voice was wobbly with emotion as I replied, 'How will we make sure he uses condoms when he gets older? What if he gets an STD?'

The look on my husband's face at that moment translated roughly as: 'You are a lunatic who has landed from another planet.'

And this is true. Forget Venus, I come from Planet Hypothetical whose population is almost exclusively female.

278

Living there is *torturous*. It is a land of angst and uncertainty. Of hopes and nightmares. Of endless potential for good or bad. It's a land of 'what if?' and self-recrimination and many sleepless nights.

Aware of my rampant post-birth hormones, my patient husband made up some garbage about how, by the time our son was old enough to need condoms, scientists would have found a way to eradicate STDs. That shut me up briefly until I had a new thought. 'One day he's going to love another woman more than he loves me . . .' And that thought was almost too much to bear. So naturally, I sobbed for my future rejected self.

Of course, the frustrating thing for future-dwellers like me is that you never get there. There's always more future until, well, there isn't. And even then, depending on your beliefs, there's more to come.

Life's possibilities are endless, which can be at once exhilarating and extremely stressful to contemplate. I've spent each of my pregnancies madly worrying about my baby's safe delivery. As soon as that blessedly occurs, I immediately begin worrying about the rest of their lives. It's exhausting.

As women, we stop living in the now early on. From the time we're girls, we're always trying on the next stage of life for size, whether it's prancing around in Mummy's high heels, writing our 'married' names during a schoolgirl crush or pestering each other with 'When will you be moving in/ getting engaged/having a baby?'

I think shopping is another manifestation of my inability to live in the present moment. Whether I'm buying food, clothes or hair products, it's all about how my life *could* be in the mythical future. It's not about cooking with what's in my fridge now, it's about buying new ingredients for the tasty meal I'd like to cook – but invariably never do. It's not about creating outfits from the clothes I already own, it's about hunting for the new pair of pants that will magically pull my entire wardrobe together – but invariably doesn't.

Ditto the mystery product that will make my hair look naturally tousled like Jennifer Aniston's. I know it's out there. I can see it in my mind.

Meanwhile, scrapbooking and Facebooking and making slideshows and celebrating anniversaries? They're about the past. I think that's why so many men forget anniversaries. It's because they excel at now, not nostalgia. And they can thank evolution for that. When a woolly mammoth was chasing Joe Caveman, there was no time to sift through hypotheticals or reflect on past mammoths. It was kill or be eaten.

Back at the cave, Joan Cavewoman had a safe and shel-
tered environment in which to gather salad greens, ponder
the future (Should we move to a better cave? Does this animal skin make me look fat or am I just knocked up again?)
and reminisce about the past (Remember that first romantic
night when he clubbed me over the head and dragged me
home by my hair?).

Grazing is another aspect to our collective inability to live
in the now. Named for the bovine practice of consuming
an endless diet of bite-sized portions throughout the day
instead of three big meals, grazing encapsulates how many
of us now live life. In small chunks, quickly and while dart-
ing around looking for something more tasty.

But why? Is it the fault of Gen X and Gen Y, the instant
gratification generations? Or is technology to blame for
giving us a billion fast ways to communicate with others
and entertain ourselves, often simultaneously. Or are we
grazing because we just don't want to commit to anything
substantial?

As British author and columnist Shane Watson observed
recently, 'If slacking defined a certain sort of 1990s mental-
ity, grazing sums up the way the majority of us now approach

everything from shopping to relationships. Not only do we hate to make a choice, but the flick-flick opportunism of our daily lives has affected our ability to live in the moment once we've made a decision. When did you last switch off your mobile while having dinner with a friend?'

Oh. Well. Um . . . does having it on silent and checking it when I go to the loo count as 'off'? It should.

The grazer is driven by one simple thing: the fear of missing something better. You know how on New Year's Eve when you were younger you avoided committing to anything until the last minute? And then on the night, you moved from bar to party, from party to club and back again, looking for the elusive Rocking Good Time aka Party Nirvana?

Well, grazing is a lot like that. It's about not committing to anything in case something better comes along. A better meal, a more relevant piece of news, a juicier bit of gossip, a more exciting invitation, a more interesting conversation. Because it just might. And if you missed it? You might die or something.

I have one friend who is on an anti-grazing crusade. 'I've given myself a personal challenge to stop multi-tasking and do one thing at a time for more than just a minute,' she explained to me in an email she insists wasn't written while watching TV. 'I'm trying to eat breakfast without reading the paper or listening to the radio. Not quite there yet. And I'm trying to drive without listening to my learn-Italian tapes or making phone calls. Next on my list is sitting and drinking a cup of tea. It's all very, very difficult but utterly exhilarating.'

Just. Drinking. Tea. Imagine that!

When I told my mum I was writing about grazing, she told me about this film she'd just seen. It was called *Into Great Silence* and here's how she described it: 'It's a documentary about monks in a monastery in the French Alps. It's a silent order and the film just follows the monks as they go about their tasks and rituals during the day. One thing at a time. No multi-tasking. No talking. And you see the seasons gradually change. I went last week and it's very soothing.' Wow. A silent movie about silent monks. AND IT GOES FOR THREE HOURS AND JOHNNY DEPP IS NOT EVEN IN IT. I would be totally cool with seeing that if I could bring my mobile. And my laptop. And a magazine and a torch. And also a friend to talk to.

At least with a movie like that I might be able to follow the plot. Generally, I find it challenging to work out what's going on in anything more complex than a Brand Power commercial.

I struggle to find anyone to watch movies with me

because of this, either in the cinema or at home. I get per-plexed easily and I interrupt a lot. 'Who's that older woman? Wasn't she on that TV show with that bald guy? Where is the other girl from before? Is that guy her brother or her boyfriend? I thought her brother died. But why was she with that other girl in the bedroom? Is she a lesbian? What did he just say? I couldn't hear. I don't understand what's happen-ing. But what did he do with his car? Is it still at the airport? With the other guy? Oh wait, what happened to the other guy? Did he die too?'

At this point, my movie companion either tries to smother me with a pillow if we're watching a DVD or silently reaches across to pinch me if we're at the movies. Add in my short concentration span and, needless to say, the prospect of watching a movie with me is about as appealing as eat-ing a bowl of toenails. Especially now that most movies are three hours long.

My short concentration span applies to other things too. Like music. I never listen to an album from start to finish any more. You? And meals. I can't be bothered with three courses. I'd rather skip the entree so I can fast-track dessert. And phone conversations. They take too long so I'd rather text. And reading. I flick through the papers in sixty seconds each morning and then check news online via Twitter a dozen times during the day. Books? They're for holidays, when time is not at a premium and my concentration span somehow temporarily expands.

The other thing I do quite obsessively on holidays is document them. Photos, movies, I never stop. Which has led me to wonder: at what point does documenting your life leave you no time to actually live it?

I'm constantly tortured by the idea that I'm not capturing family memories. That I'm failing to record all those special moments. So periodically, I go into a frenzy of photo taking, inspired by the thought of all those heart-warming occasions I'll have on film.

But here's the problem: it's hard to truly appreciate a moment when you're looking at it through a viewfinder. Or worse, forcing your poor subject to wait while you dash to get your camera, urging: 'Just do it again, exactly like before.' And then, 'Oh, silly Mummy didn't have the flash on. Can you just do it one more time? Yes, fall over spontaneously into the dog's bowl again, okay? Now wipe the Pal off your face and do it once more like the first time. Ha, ha, isn't that funny! Oh, wait, the battery is flat. I missed it. This is really the last time, I promise! Can you just wait for it to recharge?'

Apparently, the most common way to die on a mountain climb is at the summit when you lift your camera to your eye to capture the view, lose your balance and fall to your death. Is this the universe trying to tell us something?

I have a friend who decided several years ago to stop taking home movies of her children. She and her partner had realised they were spending too much time filming milestones instead of experiencing them. She remarked wryly that the kids would no doubt eventually resent them because they wouldn't have hours of childhood movies like their friends.

And this is exactly where I get stuck. I want to live in the moment but I also want to capture it. So how do you live in the present when you're trying to turn it into the past so you can look back on it from the future?

Apart from the lack of spontaneity, the biggest challenge in documenting your life is the damn time it takes. Invariably, all those photos start piling up, waiting for you to sort them into albums (real or virtual) or email them or print them or upload them to Flickr. Frequently, I am so busy downloading, uploading and off-loading months of family photos, I miss out on spending time with the family in question.

I'm not alone in my soup of sentimentality and angst. People have been observing for a while now that we are the generation who won't leave anything behind. Other than environmental damage.

I have boxes of letters and photos going back to primary school but the letters stop in the '90s and the photos stop around 2004 when life began to go virtual.

My son has half a dozen photo albums documenting his babyhood. A few years later when my daughter was born? Not a tangible thing. Yes, she has 'albums' too, but between one child and the next, this word has come to represent something entirely different – a collection of photos on my computer. Sure, there are hundreds of them but where he'll have volumes, she'll have . . . a hard disk? The idea of grabbing your photo albums in case of fire is now virtually redundant. You simply grab your computer.

A few years ago, when we were on holidays, I discovered (duh) that my digital camera also took movies. Looking for a project, because I've never been very good at just chilling, I quickly dived into the task of making a home movie. Cue obsession. Almost immediately, I fancied myself as the cinematic love child of Baz Luhrmann and Martin Scorsese. Within three days I became a bossy nightmare. If an activity wasn't going to be filmed, I didn't see the point of it. Going to watch some new Disney movie at the local cinema? How is that going to enhance *my* movie? It's dark there! No, you can't go.'

Next, I began to frog-march my family towards photogenic activities that would make for good film material: 'Let's have surfing lessons! Let's feed the neighbours' chickens! Let's dance with the Hari Krishnas at the markets!' I became quite crazed. Like one of those Club Med GOs after seventeen coffees.

Each night, I ignored my family's pleas to join them for board games or DVDS, preferring to edit on my laptop, cutting and pasting clips, mixing the soundtrack and feeling generally smug and obsessed. But wait, there's more.

Towards the end of the holiday, I decided I wasn't in the movie enough so I made Jason film me doing 'spontaneous' things like cartwheels on the beach or running into the surf. Later, he observed that every time I appeared in the film I resembled a deranged girl in a tampon commercial – running and jumping and laughing like a lunatic.

I thought I might calm down a little when we came home but I didn't. Instead, I decided my 'work' was so good it should be shared. That's how I came to bring my laptop out to dinner with friends one night soon after our return. Can't come to slide night? No matter! Because we'll bring it to you!

When my husband suggested I tour the restaurant with my laptop, showing the slide show to tables of strangers, my eyes lit up before I realised he was joking. Is there a rehab program for people who film too much? Surely its mantra would be 'step *awaaay* from the camera and focus on life'.

That sounds suspiciously like living in the now. I knew I should have finished that damn book.

However, to do that, to be able to focus on reading several pages *in a row*, I would need some alone time and, at this stage in my life, that is a rare thing indeed.

'I reckon I've been alone for maybe ten minutes this entire week,' I huffed to a girlfriend recently. I heard a sharp intake of breath before she went very quiet. 'And that includes bathroom time!'

If you have small children this will be no surprise to you. You will already know that going to the toilet or having a shower is something you do with an entourage. If you close your eyes you can pretend you're Mariah Carey. Or not.

The friend listening to me vent was trying to get pregnant and she was not happy with the direction of our conversation.

'You know, you're really not selling this motherhood thing very well . . . .' she sighed, deeply disturbed by the thought of an audience in her bathroom.

Perhaps she was right. Shower-as-spectator-sport is not one of motherhood's more appealing features. It's definitely not in the brochure. But gosh balls, I wish one of my 700 pregnancy books had mentioned that children hoover up your solitude. Everyone rants about not sleeping but nobody explains that you'll never be alone. And that's a huge adjustment. Babies in particular are unfamiliar with the concept of personal space. They're more like: 'Mummy's space is my space. Hell, Mummy's body is mine too.' This is a beautiful thing most of the time but on several occasions, I've found myself announcing, 'Mummy just needs five minutes when NOBODY IS TOUCHING HER. And that includes Daddy, okay?'

But you don't need to be a parent to suffer from a severe deficit of alone time. There's a far bigger solitude-sucker than kids and it's called 'technology'. You may have heard of it.

Along with social media, technology has pretty much obliterated solitude from our lives. It's difficult to be by yourself these days, have you noticed?

If Greta Garbo were alive now, she wouldn't be on Facebook. Or Twitter. The actress who starred in Hollywood's silent-film era and who famously said, 'I want to be alone' wouldn't have a BlackBerry. She wouldn't partake in Skypesex, and I doubt she'd use those precious seconds waiting for her skinny soy latte to SMS two friends and return her mother's call.

The only way Greta could really be alone today would be to quarantine herself from the technology of communication. No mobile, no Internet, no social media. Because if it's solitude you're after, hiding away behind a high, electrified fence just won't cut it any more. People will seep into your space via broadband and 3G and steal your solitude while you're watching TV – which is no longer a solitary pursuit thanks to texting and Twitter.

There are many, many benefits to this, of course. Social isolation is far easier to remedy, for one. But on the downside, technology has gobbled up our downtime. With the creeping expectation that we're all available to communicate 24/7, are we losing the ability to just twiddle our thumbs? Stare into space? Chill?

William Deresiewicz is a literary critic and former professor of English at Yale University. In a recent essay, he lamented the loss of solitude in our lives. 'Technology is taking away our privacy and our concentration but it is also taking away our ability to be alone,' he says. 'Though I shouldn't say taking away. We are doing this to ourselves; we are discarding these riches as fast as we can.'

For me, this is totally true. I may bitch and moan about having no time to myself, but whenever I do have a spare minute, I rush to fill it with communication. I return calls via Bluetooth while I drive and I text at every given opportunity – you can achieve many things at a traffic light or while standing in a queue. Much of this multi-tasking is just effective time management because, like most people, I always have too much to do. But I'm under no illusions. This efficiency comes at a price and that price is not having the mental space to just . . . think.

Our online life and social networks used to exist only when we were near a computer. But now, they've been emancipated from our desks and they can follow us everywhere, via text or social-media applications on our mobiles. We've managed to hungrily fill every gap in our lives with communication or the possibility of it. Some of us (me) have become addicted to being in constant contact. I get antsy if my phone is not within reach, apoplectic if my Internet goes down.

The problem with this is that precious things live in those little gaps between interactions. There's gold to be found in the periods of mental silence when we're not communicating. Creativity and insights and great ideas. Even just the ka-ching of remembering a crossword answer or the name of that restaurant you've been meaning to try. Those things can't bubble up to the surface until your head is clear and the chatter stops.

Running water is apparently very conducive to creativity and a-ha moments. It's no accident we have our best ideas in the shower. In some research labs, shower banks are installed so scientists can go and think under the water. I presume the shower cubicles have doors? With locks? I knew I should have been a scientist.

To be fair, I am able to have showers in the middle of the day too, if I want to, because several days a week I work from home. It is many people's dream to work from home. I am living that dream and I want to tell those people: it's not 100 per cent dreamy.

I left the office to work for myself several years ago so you'd think by now I'd have nailed the working-from-home thing. You'd be wrong.

In fact, I'm not even writing this at home. I'm writing it in a café where I've begun to flee with my laptop whenever possible. My son is appalled by this. He thinks people who use computers in public are showing off.

When I first told him I was working in a café, he thought I was making coffee. This was preferable in his mind to what I was actually doing – which was writing – because only embarrassing show-offs do that.

To prove his point, a few days later he called me over to watch a scene from *Family Guy* where a couple of dudes are using their laptops at Starbucks. 'I'm writing in public because I'M A WRITER,' announces one to nobody in particular in a voice dripping with self-importance, 'working on MY LAPTOP and if nobody sees me writing, then it doesn't count.'

I took exception to this. After I stopped laughing.

There are many things about working from home that delight me. The dress code is one. I am never happier than when I can work in jeans, a T-shirt and no make-up. (Oddly, I cannot write properly when wearing a dress. I have no idea why this is, so let's just file it under B for Bonkers.)

The other gigantic benefit is seeing my children through-out the day, although I will not for a moment pretend it's possible to achieve anything other than high stress levels while trying to work with small kiddies under foot or under desk. I have help with them every workday.

And even then, I struggle.

Especially since my toddler recently discovered where Mummy disappears to during the day, and now takes every available opportunity to make like a Mexican immigrant and dash across the border into the Promised Land of my lap whenever the authorities aren't watching. Try typing with a toddler on your lap. They have forty-six hands, all trying to delete your work at the same time.

This is just one example of how my work/life boundaries have slowly collapsed. Yes, it's terrific not having to waste time commuting and it's wonderful to choose your own hours. But the downside is that you're always at the office. Even when you're asleep.

And yes, it's sublime not having to deal with petty office politics or irritating co-workers but it's also isolating. Thank heavens for Twitter and the commenters on Mamamia.com.au. They are a virtual watercooler and have transformed the home-office experience.

For a long time, I didn't even have an office at home. I just had my laptop. I'd drag it around with me from room to room, trying to avoid the rest of my family. That was a disaster.

Virginia Woolfe knew this even though she didn't have a laptop. She wrote *A Room Of One's Own* in 1929, an extended essay about the importance of having a dedicated space, however small, in which to be creative. Inspired by Virginia, I then tried setting up camp in various parts of the house before establishing a desk behind the couch.

This has worked splendidly, although it hasn't fixed my tendency to procrastinate. Like many writers, I adore writing; I just hate starting. This is a problem because, at home, you must rely solely on self-discipline when your boss can't see you unstacking the dishwasher or watching daytime TV.

There is a common misconception that people who work from home watch a lot of daytime TV but it's not true. I waste time on the Internet instead.

When you're in a café, however, especially one without wireless, you can only stuff around with your latte and a communal newspaper for so long. There are no children to attend to, no dinner to prepare, no T-shirt drawer to colour-code.

The other thing I like about working in public is the

noise. Having worked in a busy office for fifteen years, I've never been the kind of writer who required silence. The opposite. I find the hum of background noise to be conducive to work.

I think this is because my formative journalistic years in magazines were spent sharing a small and windowless room with three other women. In the five years I spent in that cramped office, we were all forced to write while our workmates spoke on the phone, conducted meetings and laughed and cried through private phone calls at full volume. There was also a thoroughfare conveniently located between our desks so all the models, designers, PRs and photographers who came to see the fashion department had to traipse through the centre of our office. This happened approximately 2000 times every hour. Not much silence, no.

Perhaps this is why, when writing, I like to be surrounded by a bit of noise without having to actually interact with anyone. I guess you'd call it socially anti-social. Or living the dream.

But I don't particularly crave an office like the one I used to work in. It certainly won't be on my vision board when I get around to making a new one.

***

A few years ago I read a book called *The Secret* (which I *did* finish – huzzah!). This did not make me particularly unique or visionary. I wasn't even an early adopter of the self-help-meets-fast-food-spirituality phenomenon.

When this book became popular, you couldn't walk outside your front door without falling over someone reading *The Secret* or claiming it had changed their life. I fell over several such people and then I became one of them.

It was an interesting time. I was quite ripe for the picking, really. Receptive to the message. I was trapped in a job I loathed, my fear of flying was at paralysis stage and I had no idea what I wanted to do next. Enter pop psychology and the not new but nicely packaged proposition that if you want something badly enough, you can have it. Simply think it (Airline safety! A different job! Family adventures!) and it will be.

I had several skirmishes with one of my friends about *The Secret*. As fervently as I believed in it (I'm nothing if not gung-ho when I jump onto a bandwagon), she insisted it was crap. 'It's an appalling premise to say if you want something you'll get it,' she huffed angrily. 'What about people who lose loved ones? Did they not love them enough? What about people who die early? Did they not want to live enough?' It was a legitimate viewpoint, one she formed having watched someone she loved lose a child. I had no decent argument. There was none.

From a practical point of view, *The Secret*'s Australian author, Rhonda Byrne, encouraged you to do a few important things. Like carry a gratitude rock and touch it regularly to remind yourself to be grateful for the things you already have and those that will soon be yours. I found the perfect rock on a beach one day and carried it everywhere.

Fortunately, my rock was small enough to fit in my pocket. I was grateful for that. Unfortunately, on the day a certain TV show I was involved with premiered, I dropped my rock in the toilet. To everyone who lost their job when that show was axed a few months later, I'm so sorry. I blame the damn rock.

Still, I resolutely tried to stay positive because that's what *The Secret* demands. Negative thoughts bring with them negative realities, and heck, I didn't want those, even if my gratitude rock was now inauspiciously lost in the sewer system.

Another thing *The Secret* encouraged was creating a vision board. I took to this hesitantly at first and then with great enthusiasm. The idea is to stick up specific images of the things you want in life. If you want to travel, don't just stick up a photo of a plane. Find an image of a place you'd like to visit, even down to a specific landmark or restaurant. If you want money, write yourself a pretend cheque for a specific amount. *The Secret* brims with gushing testimonials from people who made vision boards and then years later became the proud owner of the exact house or bike or amount of money they'd pinned up.

So I got busy. I printed out images of particular locations, logos of companies I wanted to work with, people whose careers I wanted to emulate, objects I wanted to own. It was a lot like writing a list for Santa. At the last minute, I decided to sneak in a photo of myself pregnant, hoping my husband wouldn't notice. He didn't. Time passed and I forgot about my vision board.

About a year later, I took another look at my vision board for the first time in months and nearly fell over. Several of the shots I'd pinned up were almost exactly replicated in our recent overseas holiday snaps. Perhaps I'd done this subconsciously or perhaps that's exactly the point. And in the twelve months following that, pretty much everything I'd put on my vision board came into my life in some way.

I'd had job offers from two of the companies whose logos

I'd printed out. I had become a regular contributor to the third. And I was pregnant. My new book was about to be published and I had an iPhone. For me, vision boards aren't just about material things. They're not a shopping list. Even just the process of thinking carefully about what you want from your future and what images might represent those things is an invaluable exercise because it forces you to put wafty ambitions into pictures.

Of course this is the polar opposite of living in the now, isn't it? I wonder if there's a self-help book about how to resolve the conflicting instructions you get from self-help books. I'd buy that. Reading it? Well, that's another story . . .

Acknowledgements

If I had to rely on my own life, opinions and experiences alone for my writing, I'd be well and truly stuffed.

So to all the friends, family, colleagues and passing acquaintances who have allowed me to pillage their lives for anecdotes and opinions, you have my enormous thanks.

Thanks also to Tara Wynne, my eternally calm and wise literary agent; Kirsten Abbott, the publisher I was always meant to have; and everyone at Curtis Brown and Penguin.

To my beloved readers at Mamamia.com.au, thank you for providing me with such eloquent, supportive and feisty daily feedback on everything I write; and to the wonderful readers of my column in the Sun Herald and Sunday Age, who are the most loyal and vocal folk in the land.

To my inner circle of girlfriends, who I love, adore and lean on constantly, thank you for replying to my texts, meeting me for wine and pasta, and understanding that I'm crap at picking up my phone when it rings.

Finally, to Jason, Luca, Coco and Remy, who I love ferociously . . . thank you for your endless patience when I'm forever writing in my head instead of listening to what you're saying or asking me to do. I know you have to repeat yourselves a lot and I'm so sorry. I'll try harder. I promise.

Mia culpa . . . xxxxxxxxxxxx